God I Wish I Was Wearing
Tennis Shoes Right Now

Terry Nails

1st WORLD
PUBLISHING

God I Wish I Was Wearing Tennis Shoes Right Now

Terry Nails

Copyright © Terry Nails 2013

Published by 1st World Publishing
P.O. Box 2211, Fairfield, Iowa 52556
tel: 641-209-5000 • fax: 866-440-5234
web: www.1stworldpublishing.com

First Edition

LCCN: 2013910389
SoftCover ISBN: 978-1-4218-8667-1
eBook ISBN: 978-1-4218-8668-8

This material has been written and published for educational purposes to enhance one's wellbeing. In regard to health issues, the information is not intended as a substitute for appropriate care and advice from health professionals, nor does it equate to the assumption of medical or any other form of liability on the part of the publisher or author. The publisher and author shall have neither liability nor responsibility to any person or entity with respect to loss, damages or injury claimed to be caused directly or indirectly by any information in this book.

Special thanks go to the following without whose help and support this book would have not been possible: Del James for his insight and editing and for making me keep it simple. Pam Youngquist who worked with me on every aspect of the book from the very beginning. Toni Drew, Fayette Hauser and Claude Palmer who were there with all the details when I needed them. Camile Atkinson for her keen ability to find the weak points and for having the courage to point them out. Dennis McKenna for giving me the courage to write this and for his kind support throughout the day to day writing process and for contributing to the text. The late Terence Mckenna for leading the way. And last but not least my dear friend Rodney Charles for his encouragement and for being crazy enough to publish this.

Each one of our lives is but a single sentence
in the vast never ending tale we call the Universe...

Foreword

As I reflect back upon this single sentence that I call my life, I am reminded of the title of a song by one of my favorite bands the Mermen *'With no definite future and no purpose other than to prevail somehow'*. That pretty much sums up the way my particular adventure has taken shape. I've done nothing by the book so to speak. I've followed my own path and made mistakes and hopefully will continue to learn from them. There is a quote from Joseph Campbell that I think fits the situation pretty well:

"Follow your bliss. If you do follow your bliss, you put yourself on a kind of track that has been there all the while waiting for you, and the life you ought to be living is the one you are living. When you can see that, you begin to meet people who are in the field of your bliss, and they open the doors to you. I say, follow your bliss and don't be afraid, and doors will open where you didn't know they were going to be. If you follow your bliss, doors will open for you that wouldn't have opened for anyone else".

I have found that in my case at least, this is solidly true. Don't get me wrong, I wasn't aware of any of this at the time I started out. I had no noble pioneering spirit of adventure driving me. I simply went where I knew I had to go because to me there was no other choice. When I finally was able to quit drinking and doing drugs and get clean and sober it wasn't due to any great effort on my part. It was more as if the Universe as a whole decided one day that I was no longer allowed to continue with those particular patterns of behavior. **In no uncertain terms and to my great relief I was done and I had to accept that whether I liked it or not.**

I have been privileged to have met many interesting people along the way. I have been involved in many interesting and at times dangerously dumb situations. Somehow I survived these good, bad, and just plain stupid situations. I guess if all we truly have is our one small sentence to contribute to the universal tale the very least we can do is make it as interesting as possible…

Terry Nails,

near the end of the Mayan calendar 2012…

"How can I tell that the past isn't a fiction designed to account for the discrepancy between my immediate physical sensations and my state of mind?"

—Hitchhikers Guide to the Galaxy

Chapter 1

'God I wish I was wearing tennis shoes right now' I thought as I rounded the corner of Cole and Haight. As I ran into the street I was suddenly forced to retreat back on to the sidewalk by the green unmarked squad car bearing down on me in reverse. Three seconds later I felt the full 200+ pounds of offi cer Garrett as he grabbed me by the hair and body slammed me to the pavement and proceeded to choke me in an attempt to keep me from swallowing whatever he thought I had in my mouth. Too late, what I'd had in my mouth I'd already swal-lowed. In this case the items were small tightly wrapped balloons fi lled with heroin. I had long since gotten into the habit of swal-lowing whatever I had in my mouth every time I saw Offi cer Garrett. I did this for two very good reasons. Number 1: every time he saw me he would stop me and search me and number 2: he would always have to let me go - after relieving me of any cash he found - when he couldn't find anything illegal on me.

This time, however, was different, very different. I had broken my own cardinal rule which was to never, I repeat never, carry more than you can swallow! Well, when I fuck up I don't mess about.

The look of disappointment on his face when he realized that I didn't have anything in my mouth was soon replaced by a smug look of triumph when he found two ounces of heroin in my front pocket, the $1600 in my jacket and the two .25 Beretta automatics I was carrying, one in each boot.

When I saw officer Garrett jump out of the car I knew - as they say in the detective novels - that the proverbial 'jig was up'. I also knew that I didn't stand a politicians chance in a truth telling contest of outrunning him but I had to try. And thus I found myself handcuffed, crammed in the back of a squad car, and on my way to the San Francisco Police Department's Golden Gate Park station on Waller Street.

So how did I get to this place in life? How did I end up incarcerated, with three grand jury indictment sales charges against me - in the wrong name I might add - under age, dope sick as hell and searching through my own fecal matter for the balloons I'd swallowed earlier?

Well to understand this we need to go back a bit. Quite a bit actually to the rapidly receding tropical forests of Africa and follow in the footsteps of a certain group of bipedal apelike creatures which quite recently had taken to following herds of ungulate animals in an attempt to find new sources of food because of the rapid climactic changes taking place in their environment. These creatures didn't know it yet but they were on the verge of a great evolutionary step. They didn't know it yet because to them it seemed like they were on the verge of starvation. As it turns out this was in fact the key to the whole scenario. Their normal food source was rapidly disappearing. They were hungry and looking for new sources of sustenance. Basically they were trying anything and everything to see if it was edible.

Now interestingly enough one of the more abundant food sources that was readily available to them was something that falls under the heading of Copelandia bispora, a substance which readily grew from the dung of the animals that they were now following.

And as we all know if you get hungry enough you will eat practically anything.

Now one of the better-known effects of this new dietary substance is greatly increased visual acuity i.e. eyesight. This, as it turns out, is a mind bogglingly useful ability to have if you ever happen to find yourself in the role of hunter gatherer/prey. Another effect of this substance was the stimulation of the central nervous system. This produced a heightened sense of environmental awareness, dissolution of ego boundaries and increased interest in all things procreative. Or, as we say nowadays, you became horny. This in turn led to more successful hunting, more successful copulation, a bigger population, the invention of agriculture and the necessity of forming an agricultural community or city.

Along with this came the discovery of grain fermentation which in turn led to more successful copulation along with the invention of beer, taverns, and eventually AA meetings. But this was just the beginning. It also led to the development of the wheel, metal work, art, religion, war, the printed word - closely followed by the introduction of propaganda - new and more destructive ways of waging war, kingship and all the fascinating byproducts of rule by divine right such as slavery, serfdom, indentured servitude and so on and so forth.

Anyway farther down the line we have the invention or rather development of systems of thought such as philosophy, mathematics, science and certain ways of looking at the physical world, or what is known today as physics. Among the developers of the Western subsystems were Socrates, Heraclitus, Plato, Aristotle, St. Augustine, Galileo, Newton, on up to Immanuel Kant and then Einstein. This long slow process eventually led to two world wars, the splitting of the atom, the invention of the hydrogen bomb, mutually assured nuclear destruction, the Red scare followed closely by the Cold war and finally the introduction and distribution of the anti-depressant drug Prozac as a general panacea for what ails you. This in a roundabout way leads us to where we all happen to be right now. Which come to think of it is way past the point in time I was trying to get to.

Okay, the time was the early 70's. The place was San Francisco and I was in one hell of a predicament. I'd been paraded through the precinct station like some sort of a rare zoological oddity and was led into a small office where I was read the charges against me. Here it eventually came to light that I was not in fact the person known as Richard Allen 'Dickie' Peterson - whose name was on the warrants as well as the ID I had been carrying for over a year - but that I was actually an under-aged runaway named Terry.

You should've seen the utterly defeated look on Garrett's face. It was almost worth the roughing up I got from him and his partner just before they shipped me off to juvenile home. It was brilliant! I mean, Garrett was such a dick and I don't mean detective - although in fact he actually was a detective, a detective who regularly used his badge to relieve anybody he suspected was dealing of all their cash. Now don't get me wrong, not all the police officers in San Francisco were like that. In fact very few were. Most of them were straight shooters, no pun intended. The ones that were dirty, however, all seemed to be narcotics officers. Go figure.

Shortly after my sendoff by Garrett and his buddy, I was transferred to the main juvenile facility in San Francisco. This was to be my home for the next few weeks, a home where for the first few days I kept a close watch on my stool matter in an attempt to recover the balloons I had swallowed.

Later I found out I had somehow managed to scare the living shit out of everyone at this facility - staff, inmates, doctors, everybody. The reason was because I had no recollection of the fi rst week and a half at all. It was a total blank. Zip, nada, nothing. I guess I had been so sick and delirious that the staff members were concerned for my life and the other inmates were concerned for theirs. They had no idea what the hell was going on with me but they all knew one thing - they wanted to be as far away for me as they could possibly get. In situations like mine the standard medical treatment at the time was to load you down with as much Thorazine as they thought they could legally get away with. This, as it turned out, was quite a lot.

Chlorpromazine(CPZ) was first synthesized on December 11, 1950 and was marketed in the United States as Thorazine. It was the first drug developed specifically as an antipsychotic. The effect of Thorazine can best be described as a kind of temporary chemical frontal lobotomy. It was sort of like having your head opened up and chocolate syrup poured all over your brain. It sapped you of strength, will, and the ability to think above the level of say, a demented bee. One of the main side effects of Thorazine was that it caused a type of restlessness where the patient attempted to walk constantly, despite having nowhere to go due to mandatory confinement, all the while taking small shuffling steps. This side effect became known later as 'The Thorazine Shuffle', a pitifully comical sight but one that was no fun at all to participate in.

After being there for a couple weeks I was told that I had a visitor. I was then introduced to a strangely familiar looking man that turned out to be my father. He looked concerned. I just looked off into space, which is pretty much the most strenuous thing I could manage to do at the time.

Anyway the gist of our conversation was that in a few days I was to be taken to the San Francisco international Airport and put on a flight to Las Vegas where I would then be transferred to the main Clark County juvenile facility, a place I had become quite fa miliar with over the years. The flight itself wasn't too bad and the officer who accompanied me turned out to be a genuinely nice person. He even took my handcuffs off just before we boarded the plane.

Chapter 2

The flight from San Francisco to Las Vegas was short and un-eventful. However, little did I know that waiting for me on the other end of this plane ride was one of the gnarliest, most pissed off little bastards anyone could ever hope to meet. The former youth camp guard, turned Gestapo agent/juvenile parole officer Mr. Deland. He was an overachieving, tobacco chewing, over-the-top jock type that hated anybody more than 2 inches taller than he was - which as it turns out was pretty much everybody except small children. He couldn't have been more than five-foot-three. Little man complex doesn't even come close to describing what was going on with this prick.

I first came into contact with Deland at Spring Mountain Youth Camp a few years earlier and we had hated each other ever since. He had tried to make things as difficult as he could for me. After spending more time than almost anyone ever had in the history of the youth camp, he was made my parole officer.

Shortly after that I left town having never once reported to him.

And now here we were again, face-to-face. The smile on his mug warned me that I just might be in more trouble than I expected.

Deland immediately slapped the cuffs on me, admonished the officer who had accompanied me for allowing such a dangerous criminal to fly on a public airplane un-manacled and marched me off through the airport like I was John Dillinger. On the way to the juvenile facility he informed me that he had already petitioned the court to have me certified as an adult and that it was his fondest hope to have me sent to Carson City prison on the drug charges which, unbeknownst to me, would soon be dropped on the technicality that I was underage and was not the person named on the warrants. Needless to say I was pretty goddamned scared. I mean, have you ever seen Carson City prison?

Opened in 1860 and burned to the ground in 1867, then rebuilt and up till the time of this event maintained in its original Civil War era condition. The place was a bloody nightmare. The prison hosted the nation's first state-sanctioned execution by lethal gas. From 1932 until 1967 the inmates operated the "Bullpen," a stone building converted into a casino on the grounds of the 140-year-old state prison that was open to the public. Hell they found fossilized footprints of a "giant race of men" buried deep within the prison quarry. The prints they found gave rise to the legend of Homo Nevadensis - a supposed lost branch of the human evolutionary tree. All of Nevada's death row prisoners were there. It was fi lled with all kinds of mean and nasty and ugly and horrible crime-type guys! It was certainly no place for a 17-year-old.

Needless to say the time leading up to my court date was pretty damn stressful. I was facing the very real prospect of spending a lot of time locked up being a boy toy in a Nevada state penal institution. After a few days I was taken before Judge Compton - who happened to be the brother of the doctor who had been our family physician since 1956 - where they asked me a few questions, sorted through a few papers at which point the judge was interrupted with an emergency phone call.

A few minutes later I was ushered back in and told by the judge that all the charges had been dropped. I was being released into the custody of my father with the recommendation that he send me to some sort of a drug treatment facility. I'll never forget the dejected look on Deland's face when he heard the judge's decision. He had just lost his last chance to get me and he knew it. I had just dodged a large bullet and for the life of me I couldn't figure out how this had happened. I mean, even if they couldn't use the drug charges because they were out-of-state and technically no good, they had me dead to rights on parole violations. From my personal experience the state of Nevada had never let anybody go on anything ever. Yet I seemed to be walking away Scott free, but why?

The reason for this I found out later had to do with the business my father was in and the type of people who founded and ran Las Vegas.

Chapter 3

Aside from the fact that it was incredibly hot and desolate and way too far away from the ocean, Las Vegas wasn't a bad place to live in the 50's and 60's.

Our neighborhood was populated with people that either worked at Nellis Air Force Base or the Nevada test site where they tested the atomic bombs. One of our neighbors even had an underground bomb shelter in his backyard that we used to play in. All the public schools used to conduct periodic civil defense drills. These drills taught us that we were supposed to 'duck and cover' in case of a nuclear attack. In other words we were supposed to duck under our desks and cover our heads with both hands. I'm not sure what this was supposed to accomplish except maybe that it would have made it easier to find our remains by simply looking under our desks.

Vegas was still pretty small in those days and the most booming place in town was Fremont Street. You could walk up and down the street from one casino to the next carrying an open beer or a mixed drink legally. (Actually you could drive like that as well back then).

The place was lousy with casinos on both sides of the street. There was the Pioneer club, Binion's horseshoe, the Golden Nugget, the Lucky strike club, the Golden gate Hotel, the Las Vegas club, the Fremont, the mint (where my mom worked for a time as a book-keeper), the Nevada club, the California club and the Boulder club to name a few.

The strip on the other hand was fairly sparsely populated with only 14 major hotels in full operation over a 4.2 mile stretch of road in 1958.

In those days Vegas was a freewheeling town where the mob bosses ruled the day and the Rat Pack presided like royalty over the local entertainment scene. Frank Sinatra, Dean Martin and Sammy Davis Junior all had houses in the prestigious Rancho Circle area of town.

In 1966, Howard Hughes, the eccentric self-proclaimed hero of the American aviation industry and noted American financier, moved to Las Vegas, initially staying at the Desert Inn Hotel where, after refusing to vacate his room, he instead decided to purchase the entire hotel. It was in this hotel that my father began working in 1956, playing music in the Sky Room and entertaining at many of the private parties for the hotel's owners.

The original name of the casino was Wilbur Clark's Desert inn, though locally it was known as the DI. Wilbur began building the resort in 1949 and quickly ran out of money. The Cleveland mob led by Moe Dalitz cut a deal with Clark and came in and took over construction of the project. Clark became the public front man for the hotel with Dalitz remaining quietly in the background as the principal owner.

Originally Moe worked in his family's Cleveland based laundry business and began his career as a bootlegger when prohibition began in 1919 - utilizing the access he had to the laundry trucks of his family's business. He ran a leading criminal organization of Jewish American gangsters called the Cleveland syndicate who were known for their violence and criminal ways. Moe was also a longtime friend of Meyer Lansky who was one of the main archi-tects of modern organized crime, a fact which led the FBI to suspect that Dalitz played a vital role inside Lansky's powerful organization.

Dalitz developed a partnership with the Maceo Syndicate which ran Galveston and supplied liquor from both Canada and Mexico. Dalitz formed strong ties with Cleveland's Eastside little Italy community and he later merged his group with top underworld leaders from the Murray Hill and Mayfield Road area. His Invest-ments in Las Vegas began late 40s with the Desert Inn. He also ran the Stardust resort and casino for time after the death of owner and former bootlegger Tony Cordero.

Moe was a legendary character who was greatly respected and admired in town. From what little I can personally remember of him, and what I gathered from the stories that my dad told me about him, he was a big hearted guy who would do anything for you if he liked you, but was someone you didn't want to get on the bad side of. My younger brother Ted and I used to refer to him as uncle Moe, though in truth we only saw him three or four times. He owned the Desert Inn until 1967 when he sold it to Howard Hughes.

So what does all this historical nonsense have to do with me beating the rap so to speak when I went to court? Well since my father worked for Dalitz in the early days playing not only at the hotel but at his private parties as well, he decided to return the favor by helping him to keep his drug crazed idiot son out of prison. In other words, it was through the beneficent intervention of this gentlemen that I was allowed to be released into my father's custody without going directly to jail as they say in monopoly.

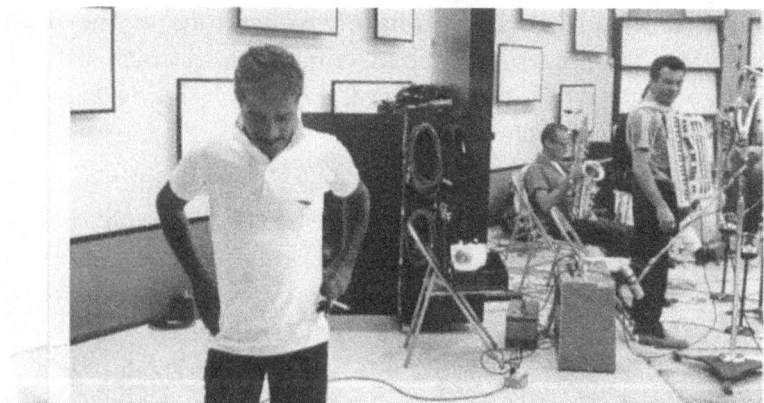

Autie Goodman sax with Sammy Davis jr recording
Photo Credit - Dad

Chapter 4

The main problem I've had growing up is that my ideas about what is important differ greatly from that of the general populace. That and the fact that I actually never managed to grow up. Grow up? I really just don't get it. I understand what it means in the general context of our society but I've never really put great stock in the values of our Western society. I've always thought that the things that society tells us are the hallmarks of success and happiness were not only archaic, unsustainable and clearly not very well thought out, but would eventually end up doing nothing but sending this technologically clever group of bipedal apelike creatures speeding headlong towards their own demise. The problem here seems to be one of focus. These creatures have been focused more on symbolic representations of life than the actual experience of life itself. This brings us to where our general points of view differ.

The gathering and collecting of the symbols of wealth, the wish to attain power and control over others at any cost, the total disregard of the importance of nature and the desire to fit in with the group even at the cost of your own sense of moral ethics have never seemed like particularly admirable ways to operate. The predicament for me has always been that I've never been able to understand why anyone would want to get involved in such a ludicrous enterprise in the first place. As Ram Das once said "it seems like such a schlock scene!" I agree! I've never been able to gather enough interest in society to allow me to appreciate the intricacies of the social game. Hence I've always looked at it more from the standpoint of an anthropologist rather than a participant.

And since all of these behaviors are aspects of what society calls "growing up" it is an action that I've been forced to abandon.

I put all this here so you'll understand when I say that "I grew up in Las Vegas" that the statement is meant more to refer to the fact that I spent much of my younger years there and not to the actual process.

I grew up in Vegas with the distinct impression that something was dreadfully wrong. Not just with Vegas but with reality itself, or rather, what passes for reality. I've talked to many people that have told me that when they were very small children, they had a very strong sensation that they didn't belong here. They felt like they'd been stranded or marooned. Sort of like this: imagine you're taking a bus trip across Europe and at one of the stops after going in to use a restroom you come out to find that not only has the bus gone but that it has taken your luggage, money, wallet and cell phone, and not only does no one in the area speak a word of English, they don't seem to be interested in communicating with you even if they could. Well, I happen to be one of those people that had that feeling. I also felt like there was something very important that I needed to remember about this place but I just couldn't put my finger on what it was. It's sort of like when you see someone whose face is really familiar yet you can't remember where you know them from or what their name is.

Aside from all that nonsense, life seemed fairly normal I suppose. My mom worked part-time as a bookkeeper for the Mint Hotel and Casino and for an outfit that sold boats and water skis. I had a brother who was 14 months younger than me whose name was Ted. Our family had a house, a ski boat, a big green 1953 Cadillac, that was soon replaced by a gold and cream colored 1957 Plymouth.

My dad was an entertainer who worked around town. Aside from the band he had that worked at the DI in the early days, he did work with Sammy Davis Junior, Billy Eckstein, Woody Herman, the Modernaires, Buck Owens, and was a member of the Four Freshmen. Generally he would leave for work around seven in the evening and returned around three in the morning.

My brother and I spent almost every Sunday with our dad at the Henderson drag strip. The man who owned the drag strip was named Oral Bendor. He lived about six houses down the street from us and every time they had a race he would give us free tickets and pit passes.

Me and my brother Ted with Grandma 1957
Photo Credit - Mom

In the early days of drag racing, the cars never did burnouts before they raced. They would just pull the car up to the starting line and wait for the guy to drop the flag then just go for it smoking the tires all the way. Because we spent so much time in the pits, we became friendly with many of the racers. Sometimes they would put me and my brother in the cockpit of the cars to steer them as they pushed them up to the starting line. We were pretty small at the time so we would just stand on the seats and turn the steering wheel when they told us to.

Ted. Terry. Kris. Jill 1963
Photo Credit - Mom

One car in particular that I remember doing this in was called the Green Monster. It was owned by Art and Walt Arfons. The thing was 20 feet long, had six wheels and was powered by a 12 cylinder Allison airplane engine. The front end of the car was painted to resemble one of the World War II fighters that the engine came out of, open shark's mouth motif and all. The thing was loud and scary and I loved it! However, the first time they actually started the car with me in it I was scared to death. In those days the crew usually consisted of just two guys and it took the two of them to start the engine. They would have to pull a couple of knobs in the cockpit, go back and fiddle with a couple of valves or something, crank a couple of levers, and would both be standing outside of the cockpit when they first fired the engine up. I was frozen with fear at the thought that I might accidentally touch something in the car that would make it take off down the track with me in it and yet strangely disappointed when they finally took me out of it.

It was about this same time that Ted and I became utterly obsessed with surfing, an obsession I still lovingly carry to this day. We couldn't get enough of it. I remember buying the first issue of surfer Magazine and how my brother and I cut it up and pasted pictures all over the walls of our bedroom. We would spend all of our allowance money on anything that had to do with surfing. If it had a picture of someone surfing on it, we would buy it. We were like surf junkies, we couldn't get enough of it. We loved surf bands. We bought records by the Chantays, Dick Dale, the Surfaris, the Tornadoes, the Ventures, the Challengers, Jim Waller and the Deltas, the Trash Men, Sandy Nelson, Jan and Dean and of course the Beach boys.

The one problem that we had with all this was that we lived nowhere near the ocean and it drove us nuts! All we wanted to do was learn how to surf so naturally we jumped at every opportunity we could in order to get to California. To us it was just a simple problem of location. All we had to do was convince the family to relocate to someplace like Huntington Beach or Redondo or even Malibu and all our problems would be solved. It soon became quite clear that there was little chance of that happening so we had to put Plan B into action.

Plan B consisted of begging and pleading with our father to take us to California with him when he worked there. Usually the begging and pleading was accompanied with behavioral modification promises that we never quite managed to pull off. Fortunately my dad was open to the idea and took us with him every chance he got. Whether he took us with him just to shut us up or he was simply trying to keep us from driving our mother insane by giving her a break from us I'll never know. It certainly wasn't because we were fun to be with. We weren't. We were a brawling squabbling nightmare.

In the meantime we contented ourselves with going waterskiing with the family and when we were not doing that Ted and I kept ourselves busy building skateboards, something that I thought I had accidentally invented when the handle of my homemade scooter fell off and I continued to ride it that way. For a while we thought that it was just he and I and a couple friends that were doing it because we'd never ever seen anyone else do it. That all changed when we saw the first picture of someone riding one in surfer magazine. They called it Sidewalk Surfing and that's all it took to send us into an intense research and development phase.

One of the main problems with skateboards at that time was that they had a tendency to throw you flat on your face because they would come to a dead stop every time the wheels came into contact with even the smallest of pebbles. Couple that with the fact that the wheels were made of solid steel and had no grip whatsoever and the experience was not so much one of sidewalk surfing but more of one that involved picking yourself up off of the sidewalk every few feet. The alchemical process involved with creating one of these vehicles was pretty straightforward. All you needed was a piece of wood, a single roller-skate, a hacksaw, a hammer and nails and in certain circumstances, wood screws and a screwdriver. The actual construction was accomplished using the principles of applied physics, though in certain cases the use of sympathetic magic proved to be quite helpful as well.

The physics part of it was fairly simple. You would take the roller-skate and cut in half with a hacksaw and then nail or screw the two pieces to the bottom of a 2 x 4. The sympathetic magic aspect of it was only used as a last act of desperation. The ritual usually took the form of my brother and I going into the house looking sad and dejected in the hopes that our father would have enough sympathy for us that he would go out into the garage and magically help us finish the project. Our initial research took the form of making longer and longer boards. The idea was to see if we could get the boards to go over the pebbles by putting more weight on the back of the board. This did keep the front wheels from skidding to a stop but it didn't keep the back wheels from doing it. Our next equipment advance came to us one day while we were watching television. In the show we were watching there was a group of people that were at a roller-skating rink and we noticed that the wheels on their skates looked very different from the ones that we had been using.

We immediately knew what we had to do.

We gathered up what was left of our allowance money, got on our bikes, road down to the roller rink, rented one pair of roller-skates and promptly walked out the back door with them. Before anyone knew it we had two new high-tech test vehicles with wooden wheels and a lot of explaining to do to our parents.

The explaining part was really pretty easy because Ted and I had become very good liars. The construction part though was complicated by the fact that we had to deconstruct the shoe skates before we could actually begin construction on the skateboards. This proved to be a lot harder than it looked but after several hours we managed to destroy the skates without causing too much collateral damage.

Our first construction attempt resulted in a board that turned the wrong way when you leaned it because we had put the trucks on backwards.

On the next attempt we got one truck on the right way and one on the wrong way, the result was a board that went sideways but continued going straight.

On the third attempt we got it right.

The first thing we noticed about the boards was that they were much quieter and turned much better than the steel wheeled ones. The next thing we noticed was that instead of the wheels stopping every time they hit pebbles, the pebbles would sometimes get stuck in the wheels themselves. The next thing we noticed was that they held on in corners a bit better and finally we noticed that every time we rode the boards the wheels would get smaller and smaller. Anyway, after a few more visits to the roller rink we finally came into possession of a couple sets of composition wheels. While they didn't actually work any better than the wooden ones, they did at least last longer.

Chapter 5

"Slow down, you're going 50 mph!"

The voice was barely audible above the roar of the wind as it ripped past my ears. The voice was coming from the open driver's window of the car that my mother was driving and the look on her face told me that she was clearly worried. The problem was I had no way of accommodating her request because at that moment I was standing barefooted on a 5 foot long piece of 2 x 4 that had 2 shoe skate trucks screwed to the bottom of it and I was too busy trying not to crash into my brother or run off the side of a cliff all the while hurtling down the road that led from the top of Mount Charleston towards, what seemed to all parties concerned, certain disaster.

For some time my parents had owned a lot near the top of Mount Charleston that they someday planned to build a cabin on. We would occasionally go up to the mountains and spend the day hanging out at the lot. It was during one of these visits that we noticed that all the roads had been repaved with brand-new incredibly smooth blacktop and that it was perfect for riding skateboards. Ted and I immediately went to work designing boards for just such conditions. What we came up with were 5 foot long boards whose length helped keep the chance of developing speed wobble and pebble skid to a bare minimum.

At first we would just cruise around but as we got used to the boards we decided to start pushing it a bit farther each time we went up there until we finally decided to try and go for it from the top. This is how Ted and I found ourselves in that predicament during our first run.

Fortunately, neither of us crashed and we made it all the way to the bottom of the mountain. We were so stoked that we coasted to a stop, all the while screaming our heads off. Our mom looked at us like we were nuts as we got back in the car to go back to the top of the mountain. She and my dad actually let us do it again on our way back home.

Anyway it wasn't until 1962 that I was actually able to get a hold of a surfboard and put it in the water. Fortunately the hotel we were staying in was right next to the ocean in Newport Beach. Unfortunately, I chose to make my first attempt at surfing at the nearest break to where we were staying and that place was called - The Wedge...

The Wedge is a big beautiful amazingly hollow, shallow breaking wedge shaped mutant wave that more often than not ends in a closeout. The beach itself is so steep and the backwash is so strong that at times it seems impossible to get back out of the water if you don't know what you're doing. I was 10 years old, the board was 10 feet long and I clearly didn't know what I was doing. It ended up being one of those bizarre situations where the worst part of the experience and the best part of the experience were one and the same.

The worst part of the experience was that I nearly drowned, the best part of the experience was that I only nearly drowned. But who cares? I was so stoked about the fact that I had been in the ocean with a surfboard and waves that I totally failed to notice that I never managed to actually stand up on it. I also failed to notice that I almost died. To me those were just minor details to be ironed out later. In my mind I was now a real surfer and that's all that counted. I triumphantly returned to Las Vegas with tales of the sea and an exaggerated sense of my own abilities as a surfer.

To me public school was an exercise in mindless drudgery that preyed on free thought and suffocated the spirit. Don't get me wrong, I love learning and I love reading. I love the process of investigation when it's applied using the true spirit of science which means keeping an open mind all the way through no matter what you may find. I love the study of the English language, philosophy, comparative religion and ancient history. Unfortunately we were taught almost nothing of this in school. Except for reading and the small bit of English grammatical structure that we were able to pick up in the process of learning to doing so, the vast majority of the curriculum seemed like it was designed for only one purpose: To make you fit in and not ask questions. To be a good little soldier and not step out of line.

Basically, I was screwed from the start. I was insatiably curious. I had an already well-developed bullshit meter and I was not the least bit interested in fitting in. The principal and teachers at the schools I went to didn't know what to make of me. My report cards consisted almost entirely of A's and F's. If I liked something I got the highest marks in the class. If I didn't like something you couldn't make me pay attention at the point of a gun. This caused so much concern that for a while it looked like I was headed for the land of the short-bus riders. Fortunately they sent me to see the school psychologist who recommended that I go see another child psychologist who would then put me through a series of tests that would enable them to find out just what the hell was going on with me. When the results of the test fi nally came back they were even more confused as to what to do with me. They decided to move me up 2 grades instead of assigning me a seat on the short bus. According to my mother this happened because the test showed that I had an IQ hovering around... well never mind, mothers always exaggerate things about their kids anyway. At any rate I had college-level reading and comprehension skills. You see, my mother taught me to read before I ever went to school and I read everything I could get my hands on. By the time I was eight years old I had already read the Iliad and the Odyssey, Gulliver's travels and regularly had my nose buried in the Encyclopedia Britannica. By age 10 I had read Paul Reps' book Zen Flesh, Zen Bones and had managed to steal a copy of the Upanishads from the library - neither of which I understood at the time but enjoyed immensely. So I guess it's not surprising that I found school to be stupefyingly incomprehensible and unbearably boring.

The funniest thing to me was that the school board actually got mad at my mom for teaching me to read at such a high level. Fortunately the fates were smiling upon me and I was not forced to endure the vagaries of public school life much longer. Through an act of divine intervention on the part of the Clark County juvenile court system I found myself being magically removed from English class wearing a brand-new pair of handcuffs in the middle of my eighth grade school year, never to return.

Chapter 6

My immediate circle of friends consisted of Steve Merket, Jim Godfrey, Mike Majors, Jay Hill, Richard Buckley, Glenn Wheeler and my closest friend, Elaine Murray a blue eyed, pale skinned pixie with long dark hair that reached several inches past her slender waist. Aside from the fact that we all liked the same music, we all hated school and would regularly ditch our respective schools together to go hang out at Glenn's house to listen to music all day. Steve, Jim, and I were still in junior high school. Mike, Jay, Richard, Elaine, and Glen were all in high school. Out of our small group Richard and I were the only showbiz kids, my dad being a nightclub entertainer and studio musician. Richard's dad was the famous hipster comedian, Lord Buckley. We were all pretty much rock 'n' roll freaks who loved to go see live bands play.

In Vegas at that time there was a teenage nightclub called the Teen Beat Club that occupied an amazingly unattractive windowless single story cinderblock building reminiscent of a WWII military storage facility. Surrounded by nothing but asphalt and empty desert, the club, located at 4416 Paradise Rd. was one of the first night clubs to cater exclusively to teenagers. It opened in 1962 and featured bands from Southern California and the local Las

Vegas area. When the club opened, the Teen Beats who played mostly surf-oriented music, were the house band. The Lords, a local rhythm and blues band featuring a Mick Jagger type singer named Fred Cole and a keyboardist who called himself John the German, frequently played there as well. I first met John the German with KENO radio DJ Jeff Colson at a station event in Las Vegas. John was dressed like Sonny Bono from the early days and his hair was so long and straight and had so many different colors in it that my brother and I figured he had to be wearing a wig. Ted and I were pretty disappointed with the whole affair because both the DJ and the German seemed kinda' squirrelly and were quite full of themselves.

The three top local rock bands in Las Vegas at that time were the Scatter Blues (who I had taken to helping out as a half assed roadie during gigs), the Sioux Uprising and the Weeds (Fred Cole's new band). All of them were very good bands but the Scatter Blues were definitely the top of the heap as far as we were concerned. It was while hanging out at the Scatter Blues house one night that I was first introduced to marijuana. I got so high and felt so bad that when I got home I actually told my dad what I'd done. He told me to go wait for him in my room. When he finally came in he was carrying a chair and I actually thought he was going to beat me with it. Instead he sat down in it and started telling me stories about how he and his friend Russ used to smoke pot before he met my mom. He told me how they had both been kicked out of a theater for going into hysterics while watching a roadrunner cartoon. Another time they decided to go get breakfast after a gig at two in the morning. They both ordered bacon and eggs when the plates came the food was arranged in such a way that it looked like a face and they busted out laughing so hard that they got kicked out of the restaurant. He told me that it was about this time that he and Russ decided not to smoke pot ever again.

Besides the local bands that played at the club, a few of the Hollywood bands would occasionally come in and play as well. Bands like Love, the Standells, Peanut Butter Conspiracy, and the Outsiders all played at the teen beat club. It was when the band Love was playing in town that I thoroughly managed to scare the shit out of my mother. The guys were in town for a couple days and for some reason only had one hotel room between them so I brought them over to our house to relax and take showers. No harm in this since my mom was supposed to be gone all day.

We were all out in the backyard except for the guitar player John Eccles because he was in my mom's bathroom taking a shower. It's about this time that my mom returned home unannounced and early. She walked into her bedroom and found a 6 foot two black man wearing only a towel and a Beatle haircut standing in the middle of her bedroom trying to get dressed. She let out a scream that could be heard all the way to Fresno! It scared poor John so bad I thought he was going to have a heart attack. I ran in and quickly explained what was going on. Mom felt so bad for scaring him that she offered to feed everybody.

It is somewhere during this time period that my friends and I decided to pool our money and get an apartment near the Sahara Hotel down by the strip. We were all selling small amounts of really bad pot by that time so we had extra money. None of us actually lived there at first. We just used it as sort of a clubhouse, though I believe Mike moved in later on. We were all too young to rent the apartment for ourselves so we had Glenn's older brother Wayne rent the place for us. We then proceeded to furnish the place with electric beer signs, flashing street signs, a spool coffee table and a couple of old mattresses.

Jay and I had been hanging out quite a lot ever since his family had moved into the house right across the alley behind my parent's house. Jay was a really nice clean-cut guy who came from Texas with his own car and about 10 pounds of shitty pot.

One night Jay and I were out cruising around when we decided to check out a party in our neighborhood. The party was at 308 Crest-line. My family's housewas just down the street at 208 Crestline.

Jay and I parked the car in the front and went inside to check out Fred Cole's new band the Weeds who were playing the party. While we were inside, one of the older girls from the neighborhood climbed into the front seat of Jay's car in order to use his cigarette lighter. At about the same time the police showed up on a noise complaint call. The girl sitting in Jay's car smoking a cigarette accidentally flicked her cigarette ash on one of the officers walking by. The officer, looking very annoyed told her to use the ashtray. With the officer standing there looking at her, she pulled open the ashtray, spilling the 2 or so ounces of pot that was stashed in it all over the front seat of the car. Next thing I knew Jay was handcuffed in the back of a police car and the cops were inside looking for me.

I immediately bolt out the back door, over the fence, and started running as fast as my little bare feet could carry me. I ended up about a quarter mile out in the desert where I waited an hour or so to see if anyone was looking for me. When they didn't, I snuck over the back fence at my parent's house and slinked into my bedroom where I spent one of the most paranoid evenings of my life.

I spent the next week or so looking over my shoulder expecting the police to show up at any minute and haul me off downtown for questioning. Miraculously this didn't happen and even more miraculously Jay gets off with a warning and informal probation. In hindsight it should've been obvious to us that something was up, but being dumb kids we just figured that we had gotten lucky.

This illusion however was shattered when Jay was asked to round us all up and bring us down town to speak with his acting proba-tion offi cer Moon Mullins.

Upon arrival at Mullins' office we were treated to an audio high-light reel of the juiciest conversations that had taken place in our apartment. They had everything; underage drinking, under age boys and girls participating in adult activities, even recordings of us taking LSD - which by the way was still legal at the time. As it turned out the police had been following us around, occupying the apartment right behind ours and had our apart-ment bugged. The scariest part of the whole experience was that Mullins didn't say a word to us. He just stared at us as we listened to the tape.

When it was over he told us to go home. It was within a few days of this incident that Steve Merket and I decided it was time to leave town.

Steve and I had been hanging out and ditching school together since 3rd grade. Elaine was my best hanging out and talking friend and Steve was my best sneaking out the window in the middle of the night and getting into trouble friend. We did all the normal things young males do when they are unsupervised. We got drunk for the first time together, took acid for the first time together, smoked our first cigarette together and in our spare time ran a small time bicycle theft ring specializing in Schwinn Stingrays.

We hatched our spur of the moment plan one night when we were hanging out at the Teen Beat club watching Scatter Blues play. The logic upon which this brilliant plan was constructed went something like this: either the police are going to put us away or our parents are going to kill us. Either way we're in deep shit so what have we got to lose?

We walked across the street, stuck out our thumbs and were soon picked up by a truck driver who had a less than healthy interest in young boys. Fortunately there were two of us and we were able to fend the guy off long enough to get over the California border where we jumped out of the truck at the first opportunity. By three in the morning we were in San Bernardino and by 5:30 in the morning we were in the Fontana jail where we were held in detention there until we were shipped back the Las Vegas. Upon our return Steve and I were forbidden to see each other which only made us more determined to hang out together.

We were soon planning our next escape attempt and this time we decided to wear shoes, something we overlooked the first time. This time we made it all the way to the Sunset strip in Hollywood and managed to avoid capture for a couple weeks. At least I did. Somehow, I lost Steve on the first day.

I'd spend the daytime panhandling and selling copies of the LA Free Press. At night I'd go down to a club called the Hullabaloo where I saw the Buffalo Springfield, Love, The Byrds, Clear Light, and many other bands play. If I couldn't scrounge enough money to get into the Hullabaloo, I'd go up the strip and hang out around Pandora's Box and the Fifth Estate looking for a place to crash or for the next party.

It was while I was on one of my forays to this area of the strip that I was picked up by the police during a curfew sweep and taken to the main Los Angeles County juvenile facility. This was an eye-opening experience to say the least. The place was huge, under-maintained and populated by the most bizarre collection of human beings that I've ever come across - guards included.

Because I had long hair the booking sergeant thought it would be funny if he assigned me to something called unit J. It turned out that unit J was where they kept all the underage drag queens, transvestites and homosexuals. I was pretty intimidated at first because I'd never been around that group of people before and didn't know what to expect. Needless to say I was pretty scared until one of them came over and introduced herself/himself and told me to relax, that I didn't have anything to worry about. The cops were always putting straight kids with long hair in the gay tank. For some reason they thought it was funny. It was probably the safest place to be in the whole facility. Here I also learned that the gay stereotype is total bullshit. These people were not soft. They had to be tough because homophobic idiots were always picking on them. I've seen more than one redneck tough guy receive the surprise of his life when he got his ass kicked by the effeminate little guy he had just been picking on.

Chapter 7

Upon my not so triumphant return to Las Vegas, I once again found myself as a guest of the Clark County juvenile court system. I was kept in custody until my initial court appearance. I was informed by the judge that I was being made a ward of the court because I had been deemed to be incorrigible. Shortly afterwards I was released into the custody of my parents and sent back to school and told that I would be apprised of my upcoming court date whenever they got around to figuring out exactly when it was going to be.

As it turned out, they never bothered letting me know anything. They just showed up one day in the middle of the school year, slapped the cuffs on me and escorted me to the juvenile court building where I was then told by the judge that I was being sentenced to Spring Mountain youth camp until further notice. In one fell swoop I lost my freedom and became an outlaw legend in the annals of Garside Junior high school. In my own mind anyway.

Before my sentencing, what little time I spent at school became a running battle between myself and the vice principal. I spent so much time in the principal's office that I actually started the think it was my homeroom. I was called to the office for everything from dress code violations to having long hair and wearing taps on my boots. When the school called my parents to complain about the length of my hair, my parents pointed out that they didn't think the length of someone's hair had anything to do with their ability to learn. When they threatened to suspend me for having long hair, my mother pointed out that that was exactly what I was trying to get them to do, so in the end they left me alone about my hair. As it turned out the length of my hair was soon to be a nonissue because very shortly I was to have none.

It was during the last part of my soon to be discontinuous public school education that I had the good fortune of being assigned to the classroom of a teacher named Alvin Meinhold who had a profound impact on my life. Mr. Meinhold was that rarest of creatures - a teacher who thought that the current method of teaching was in fact bad for children. He thought that public school didn't so much teach children how to think as what to think. I agree.

Mr. Meinhold was also a strong opponent of the war in Vietnam. He was articulate and compassionate. His views were based on sound and clear observations. He taught us to ask questions and not accept everything that we were told as being true. Needless to say he was a controversial figure among the faculty and the Clark County school district. Some of the student's parents went so far as to pull their kids out of his classes. The ones who stayed loved him. I don't recall him ever once using a standard textbook to teach his class. He taught us by reading from the classics, the newspaper and listening to albums.

Things began to get tense at school when during one of the school assemblies, Mr. Meinhold and several of us refused to salute the American flag in protest of the war in Vietnam. This led to calls to our parents with threats of suspension from school and the school board giving Mr. Meinhold an indefinite leave of absence. As it turned out the action on the part of the school board was constitutionally illegal and he was allowed back shortly afterward.

Chapter 8

I spent the time between my sentencing and my arrival at Stalag 13 (Spring Mnt Youth Camp) at the newly completed juvenile detention center trying to fi gure out a way to escape. As it turned out this was a lot easier than I thought it would be.

One day I noticed that the double doors at the end of the hallway on the boy's side were only locked to each other and not to the door frame by the vertical sliding bars as usual. I rounded up three of the guys that were waiting to be transferred to the camp along with me and told them I had a plan that might just get us out of there. It went something like this: we'd wait until there was a minimum of guards in the rotunda area to make our move. I would run down the hallway and push down the double bars that released the vertical bolts from the frame of the door. When I was halfway down the hallway one of the other guys would start running right behind me and hit the doors at a dead run with both feet in a sort of flying leap motion, which is exactly what he did.

The doors came open so easy that the kid who hit them behind me went flying through and landed about 12 feet out in the court yard beyond them.

With these doors now open we had full access to the still unfinished recreation area that was surrounded by a 10 foot-high chain link fence which had not as yet had its compliment of barb wire added to the top of it. Next thing I know I'm caught up in the scramble of 26 guys all trying to get over the fence at once. 25 of the 26 made it over the fence and quickly disappeared into the surrounding desert. Unfortunately I was never much of a climber and got caught before I could affect my own escape.

I was roughly and unceremoniously escorted back to my cell where I spent most of my remaining time in lockup. I was still in lockup when they brought in the last of the 23 of the original 25 guys who made it over the fence two weeks before. Two of the guys were never recaptured. I felt pretty good about that.

Chapter 9

Welcome to Spring Mt. Youth Camp! From the look of the place in the brochures it could have easily be mistaken as a holiday camp for kids. It was nestled serenely in the middle of the mountains. It had a swimming a pool, nice clean dorms and a small working farm. I arrived at the camp with a group of several other boys and to no one's surprise we quickly found that the camp was run along the lines of a Marine Corps boot camp. They took our belongings, shaved our heads and issued us camp clothing and quickly got down to the business of verbally abusing us.

We were first taught to stand at attention, to address everyone as Sir or Ma'am, and how to stand for inspection. Next we were taught how to G I a building - a particularly intense process that involved the use of toothbrushes to clean the floors - and how to do 500 reps of every single callisthenic known to man.

I got my first inkling that something wasn't right with the place when I noticed that some of the boys were not returning to their bunks at night but were instead spending the night up in the counselor's area. I further noticed that these boys were receiving special privileges and would sometimes leave the camp with the director and not return until the next day. I also noticed that, far from doing their allotted mandatory six-month stay these boys were being released within two or three months of their arrival.

When I asked one of the boys what was going on up at the cabins he got a sheepish look on his face and refused to look me in the eye or say anything. He finally told me that he couldn't say anything because he was afraid he'd get in trouble.

Well, acting like the young crusader for social justice that I imagined myself to be I told my mother what was going on at the camp and what my suspicions were. This led my mom to start asking embarrassing questions around town. The result was that shortly afterwards the camp director quietly disappeared in the middle of the night with most of the camp's funds never to be seen again.

A few days later I was brought into the main office to talk to the new camp director and a couple of other people that I assumed were officials from the juvenile court system. I was asked to tell them everything that I knew along with what I'd seen and everything that I'd learned from the other boys. At the end of the meeting I was told - in no uncertain terms - not to mention any of this to anyone, period. Far from ingratiating myself with the remaining staff members at the camp, the incident only succeeded in branding me as a troublemaker - a label that was to be the hallmark of my remaining time at the camp.

From my personal experience I would say that there are only three types of guys who end up working in youth camps. The first are guys that are genuinely interested in trying to help the kids out. The second type is usually failed jocks with control issues. The third type can be most easily described by the word "Pervert". Unfortunately it's hard to tell just what category a guy falls into until after he's been hired. I'm happy to say that after the initial incident, everybody who worked at the camp fell into category number one with a couple of exceptions.

Mr. Diener was a guy who obviously had serious issues. He was always talking about stuff like penises and how babies jacked off.

When he lost his temper he would start ranting and actually foam at the mouth. Needless to say he didn't last too long.

Another creep was named Mr. Mortensen. It was rumored that he was a college sports player of some sort who'd been kicked out for points shaving.

He was a clean-cut well-spoken devious lying thief. He used to love to have guys stand at attention and then slap them very hard in the face for no visible reason. It was actually against the law for any of the counselors to strike the juvenile detainees. He knew it and he didn't care. When a group of us got together and confronted him about this behavior in front of the camp director he denied it. Afterwards he proceeded to single each one of us out for extra duty and stepped up his program of physical abuse. This guy was a dirt bag, no question about it. He lasted at the camp far too long for my liking.

For the most part everyone else who worked at the camp was okay. Even Mr. Deland, who was a hard-nosed fascist type with a Napole-onic complex, was basically honest. Mr. Aragon was a hard-working straight shooter with a good sense of humor. Mr. Cahill, whose nickname was 'Crash', represented a hard drinking partier who showed up on time and got the job done no matter how bad he felt. Mr. Minor was a professional boxer who took it into his head that he could toughen me up by teaching me how to box. He even went so far as to book me a couple three round fights at the Silver Slipper Hotel in Las Vegas. I hated boxing.

Mr. Gines was the man who kept the camp running and fully functioning on a day-to-day basis. He did everything. He graded the roads, fixed the roofs, kept the sewage system fully functioning, ran the garbage crew and was a full-time counselor. Towards the end of my time there he was the camp director. He was honest, open-minded, very hard-working and had a wicked bullshit meter. He is one of the people that I've respected most in my life.

Jerry Geneche, aka Mr. 'G' was our football coach. He looked like a shorthaired, redheaded version of Frank Zappa, facial hair and all. He had a high-pitched voice, a bad temper and he worked us really hard. He was a very good coach.

Last but not least there was Mr. O'Neil - Mr. 'O' for short. Mr. O was a short roundish black man who had more coolness in his little fi nger than anyone I've ever met. If you picture a dark skinned cherub wearing a stingy brim hat, dark Ray Bans with a pencil thin mustache and a soul patch, smoking non-filtered Kools and wearing two-tone shoes then you'll have a pretty good idea what Mr. O looked like. This guy was John Shaft, Dolomite and Dizzy Gillespie all rolled into one. I absolutely loved the man.

After being at the camp for a while I was made a trustee and given the job of taking care of the farm animals. Being a trustee meant that you didn't have to show up for the normal work crews. You would basically get up early, eat before everyone else and head out to your job. You then came in for lunch, went back to work and only came back for dinner. It also meant that you didn't have to go to bed at the same time as the other guys and that you could go pretty much anywhere in the camp unsupervised.

It was during one of these after-hour forays that I noticed Mr. Mortensen had moved his car from the lower parking lot and parked it behind the mess hall. As I watched, the prick loaded his car up with boxes of food and a side of pork from the kitchen. While I was standing there watching the proceedings I was joined by the two other camp trustees - Fat Giles and Hancheque.

The problem with the whole episode - aside from the fact that Mortensen was stealing food from the camp - was that the camp was broke. We were running out of food fast. Ever since I'd gotten there, the camp had been struggling along because of that first director who had disappeared with all the camp funds. It had gotten so bad that I'd been forced to slaughter almost every single one of the farm animals that I had been taking care of just so the guys would have something to eat. By the time all was said and done Mr. Gines and I had killed and dressed over 200 chickens, 4 goats, 3 giant nearly rogue hogs, 20 or so ducks and the 2 peacocks we had. It was one of the most heartbreaking experiences that I've ever had in my life and here I fi nd Mr. wonderful stealing what little food we have left.

Right then and there we all three decided that we would tell the camp director what we had seen and that we would all back each other up no matter what.

The next morning I went to Mr. Gines - who was now the camp director and told him about the previous evenings events. A couple days later all three of us were brought together to confront Mr. Mortensen. When Mr. Gines asked the other two guys to corroborate my story they both just stared down at the ground and refused to say anything.

Mortensen just sat there staring at me with a big smug shit eating grin on his face.

Two weeks later Fat Giles and Hancheque were released from the camp a month and a half early on the recommendation of Mortensen. I, on the other hand, got an extra three months on his recommendation.

Fortunately Mr. Gines saw through the whole charade and a month later Mortensen was sent packing because of a little incident that took place on his watch that I am proud to say I helped plan.

Chapter 10

Not too long after I arrived at the camp my good friend Mike Majors arrived there as well. He, like myself, had also been deemed incorrigible by the court. He arrived with another friend of mine named John Fisher who had been involved in the juvenile home escape with me. Both of these guys as it happened were picked to fill the trustee vacancies that were left by the two guys who had been released early on Mortensen's recommendation.

Mortensen had been promoted to head counselor during his shifts which for most of the guys in the camp only served to make things even more intolerable. His actions were erratic, his decisions were arbitrary and he was a control freak. He loved to punish the entire camp every time there was even the smallest infraction of the rules by any one of us.

I must point out that this is not something that the other counselors did. Reprimands and punishment were normally meted out on an individual basis. Mortensen on the other hand liked to run the place more along the lines of a WWII German POW camp. Well if he was going to treat us like prisoners of war, we were going to start acting like prisoners of war and the first duty of every prisoner was to try to escape!

Now to set the stage you have to understand that the camp was nearly 50 miles from the nearest town by road and about 35 miles as the crow flies straight across the desert. The story they told us at the camp was that if anyone ever tried to escape they would die of thirst before they ever got to town. In other words you would have to be pretty desperate to try it. Well both Mike and John were feeling pretty desperate right about then and wanted out of the place at any cost. The reason for this was that they had just gone up before the review board and been turned down for release at the end of their six-month period. I myself had already been there quite a bit longer than the usual six-month stay. In fact, I had been there longer than everyone else in the camp except for that one guy who had accidentally killed his girlfriend. With the six month limit a seeming thing of the past , Mike and John now had no idea how much longer they were going to have to be there and they weren't the least bit interested in finding out.

The plan was this: we would get up a little earlier than usual for our trustee jobs, grab a couple containers to fill with water and scout the area for a good place to stash them. Then we would come back for lunch where John and Mike would take as much food as they could carry for the trip. This part was easy because John was the kitchen trustee and had access to the storage room. They would then take off and head for Red Rock canyon right after lunch and try to put as much distance between themselves and the camp as possible before dinner time.

As soon as they got out of the camp, John decided that instead of heading towards Vegas he was going to head for the California border. Mike, not knowing anyone in California wasn't too fond of the idea and decided to keep the original plan. My job was to cover for them as much as possible. If anyone inquired about their whereabouts I would say that I had just seen them up in the counselor's area or some other spot around the camp so that no one would get suspicious. The Escape was originally supposed to take place the week before but Mortensen had been out sick for a few days so we waited for him to come back before implementing our plan.

As it turned out no one asked where they were and no one even noticed that they were gone until it was time for lights out. Then all hell broke loose. Mortensen threw a hissy fit! He was at a total loss as to what to do about the situation. He mustered all the boys in camp and had us stand at attention in our skivvies while he tried to find out what we knew about it.

I tried not to laugh. Really I did, but I was enjoying the spectacle so much I just couldn't help myself. Truth be told, the guys could barely contain themselves they were so stoked. It was even better than the one fair football game that we won as a junior varsity team. I say fair, because all the schools in town thought they should teach us bad boys a lesson by fielding their first string varsity teams and kicking the shit out of us.

Anyway, Mortensen got it into his head that I had something to do with it and took me in the office and grilled me about it. At first he threatened me saying that I would be there for another year if he found out I had anything to do with it. Next he tried to buddy-buddy me with promises of release. Finally he resorted to begging. I just looked him straight in the eyes with as much contempt as I could muster, and repeated over and over again: "I don't know anything about it; I don't know anything about it." He knew I was lying and I knew he knew. I also knew that there wasn't a Goddamn thing he could do about it.

A couple weeks later they dragged Mike back to camp. They caught him two days after the initial escape but had kept him in town trying to get information about where John was and who had helped them. I wasn't in the least bit worried. I knew that no matter what they did Mike would never give up any information. Things were very different back then.

The best thing about our little enterprise was that John got away completely. He made it all the way to California and they never caught him. To me that made the whole thing worthwhile. That and the fact that two weeks later Mortensen was let go. The last time I saw him his car was parked behind the kitchen and he was loading it full of food. He then headed off down the long dirt road towards town never to be seen again.

A few months later I was released and placed on juvenile parole.

Chapter 11

Upon my return to Las Vegas, I was met by Ted and a group of friends bearing gifts of psychedelic posters and LSD. It was decided that rather than having me spend my first night at home, I should instead go with them to Red Rock Canyon where we would all take the LSD. And that we did! The night was warm. The moon was full. And the acid was by Owsley. It doesn't get any better than that when you're with people you love.

Ted and I had taken acid together many times. We always had a great time. My little brother was such an amazing kid. One time during my stay at the camp my mother had gotten ill and was in the hospital. Needless to say I didn't expect any visitors so I was quite surprised when a counselor came up and got me on visiting day and told me that someone was waiting for me in the office.

When I got to the office, there was my 11-year-old brother, with hair almost to his shoulders and holding the brand-new Hendrix and brand-new Doors albums. As we walked outside towards the visitor's area I asked where mom was and he told me she was still in the hospital. I asked him how he got there and he said 'I drove'.

"What do you mean drove" I asked?

"Mom wasn't home so I took her car and drove up here to see you and bring you a couple of albums" he said. I was so blown away I didn't know what to say. I mean, an 11-year-old kid driving 50 miles all by himself! I just gave him a big hug and we went and hung out in the visitor's picnic area where we sat there talking until it was time to go. Just before he left, he slipped me a couple packs of camels and I watched this 11-year-old kid who could barely see over the steering wheel get in our mom's car and drive away.

Anyway, that night at Red Rock turned into a three-day marathon campout with our friend Tony Tinfoil driving his bright yellow '49 Desoto back and forth into town getting supplies. It was some-time shortly after this that Tony introduced me to a very attractive young lady of about 24 that I immediately took a shine to, and she to me. Turns out she had her own apartment a few blocks off the strip and she invited me over for the evening. After I got there things progressed quite rapidly and went far better than I possibly could've imagined.

It was every 15-year-old boy's dream come true.

In the morning she got up, cooked me breakfast, told me to help myself to anything in the house, kissed me, locked me in her apartment and then went off to work. I didn't think anything of it at first because I was enjoying myself too much to think about going anywhere. When she got home that night, she cooked us dinner. We drank some wine and got right back into bed with each other. The next day the same thing happened and the same thing the day after that.

After about four days I'd had enough, not of her, but of being locked up so I opened the window in the bedroom, grabbed hold of the rain gutter, climbed down the side of the building and split. A few hours later I was picked up by a police car and taken back to her apartment where she was waiting for me with her mother.

It seems that she told the police I was an underage runaway and that she had custody of me. I looked at her shaking my head and told the police she was nuts and said "my name is Terry, I've just been released from Spring Mountain Youth Camp and I live at 208 S. Crestline Dr. with my mother and father". She started crying and I high tailed it out of there as fast as I could. Too bad really, if she hadn't locked me up I would've never thought of leaving.

A few days later, Steve, his older brother Mike and I went to the National Guard Armory to see a concert. There was a really excellent R&B band all of whom were Native Americans. Also on the bill were an LA band called the Seeds and Country Joe and the Fish from the San Francisco bay area. The concert was great and we all hung around afterwards and helped Country Joe tear down their equipment and get it loaded on the truck.

We asked them where they were heading next and they said they were doing an outdoor festival somewhere around Newport Beach. We asked if we could tag along and to our surprise they said sure, why not. So Steve and I jumped in the back of the equipment truck, followed by brother Mike in his pickup, and we all headed for the Newport Pop festival, where I once again lost Steve within the first 2 days. Go figure.

Chapter 12

The Newport Pop Festival featuring: the Grateful Dead, the Jefferson Airplane, Quicksilver, Canned Heat, Sonny and Cher, Electric Flag, the Paul Butterfield Blues Band, Eric Burdon and the Animals, Charles Lloyd Quartet, Blue Cheer, Iron Butterfly, Lee Michaels, The Illinois Speed Press, Things to Come, The Chambers Brothers, Steppenwolf, James Cotton, the Byrds, Alice Cooper, Tiny Tim and several other bands.

It took us a lot longer to get to the festival than we expected, mostly because it had been moved from its original location to an adjoining area and we had a hard time finding the place. When we finally got there we learned that everything was running behind schedule. Steve, Mike and I pitched in and started helping with the set up. We barely left the stage for the next three days as we had somehow become part of the stage crew.

The actual stage surface was designed like a giant Lazy Susan that was divided down the middle. Basically when the first band went on stage, we would load the next bands equipment onto the backside of the stage so when the first band was over we would rotate the stage, plug-in everything, and when that band started playing, we would tear down the first bands equipment and start loading the next bands equipment in its place. This meant there was a minimum of delays during the show and almost no time for the stage crew to take a break.

The easiest load in was Charles Lloyd. The toughest load in was the Grateful Dead. It's because of this particular gig that I break out in a rash every time I see a Fender Twin Reverb amp. The Dead had what seemed like a semi truck full of Fender Twins weighing over 100 pounds each.

The best thing about the gig was that I got to know a lot of the musicians as well as one of the most amazingly insane characters I've ever met in my life - a grouchy unpredictable madman who became my lifelong friend, photographer Jim Marshall.

Even after each band played, they would stick around for the rest of the shows so most of them were on or around the stage a lot of time. It was really pretty cool because some of the band members would pitch in and help us set up from time to time. It really was like one big family.

The first act was an unknown freak show of a band called Alice Cooper. Frank Zappa managed to get them booked at the festival even though they had no album and no following. They looked about as out of place at that festival as a turd in a fruit salad. They sounded just as good. Admittedly they were the first band so the sound system hadn't been worked out yet. The fact that they came on at 10 o'clock in the morning in nearly 100° weather, wearing fur coats, makeup and items of women's lingerie didn't help the crowd's reception of them.

After Alice Cooper, things got down to the business of good straight ahead rock 'n' roll. Aside from the cleanup problem we had that was caused by the giant pie fight that David Crosby started with the Jefferson Airplane at the end of the second day, everything went fairly smoothly. It was pretty funny actually. Where they came up with 250 pies I'll never know.

While I got to hear all of the bands, I was only able to watch them for a few minutes between setups. Things were kinda tough at first because even if I found the time to go get some food, I had no money with which to buy it. Fortunately, James Gurley of Big Brother, Gary Duncan the guitarist of Quicksilver and the Grateful Dead crew guys made sure that I had food the rest of the time.

When the show was over I hung around and helped tear down the stage while trying to figure out what I was going to do next. I lost Steve right after the pie fight and found out that he decided to go home. As for me I knew I couldn't go back to Vegas. I'd missed my first parole date. Anyway I was on a mission! A mission to find out just what the hell was going on here, you know, on the planet.

I managed to thumb a ride into Hollywood and got a hold of some friends of mine from Las Vegas that were in a band called the Sioux Uprising. While I was away at the vacation camp for wayward children, they had relocated to Los Angeles and were now living in a house up on N. Vine Street.

The house was a slightly run down white wooden 1920s two-story job that had about six bedrooms. I stayed in one of the guest rooms for a few days with this beautiful little girl that I met the first day I was there, taking LSD and barely getting out of bed the whole time.

After a few days I headed to Manhattan Beach to try and do a little surfing. My first day there I met a guy named Gary who said he was the lead guitar player for a band called Pacific Gas and Electric. I needed to make a little money and he had a bunch of acid he wanted to get rid of so I hung around for awhile and sold acid for him. I borrowed a surfboard and spent a couple hours a day in the water attempting to hone my wave riding skills but mostly I hung around the boardwalk selling acid and trying to avoid the police.

The cops had been getting pretty weird lately and had recently taken to asking you for your draft card instead of your driver's license. Fortunately I was able to trade a couple tabs of acid to a guy for his draft card which made things a whole a lot easier for me.

A few days later armed with my new identification and a little bit of cash, I stuck out my thumb and headed for San Francisco.

Chapter 13

One of the more interesting aspects of the so-called counterculture experience was the extent to which the United States government was involved. It is a very well documented fact that the US
military and CIA had been involved in a far-reaching program
designed to determine if psycho-active agents could be used as an
effective tool of war.

In the early 50s the military intelligence community began actively
looking into the possibility of using LSD as a sort of mind control substance that could be used as a super truth serum.

When a double agent named Jozef Cardinal Mindszenty was tried
for treason in Russia, intelligence sources noticed that Jozef seemed
to be really fucked up or as some would say quite heavily drugged.

The conclusion on the part of the US agents monitoring the trial
was that he had been drugged into testifying for the Russians.
Fearing that they were falling behind the Russians in the area of
mind control, the CIA launched an extensive decade's long research
program focused on the use of LSD.

During the 1950s and 60s elements of the US government
conducted clandestine experiments on American citizens. These

citizens included college students, drug addicts, veterans, active soldiers and sailors as well as mental patients. They also conducted experiments on willing subjects as well through hospital volunteer programs. It was through one of these volunteer programs that the author Ken Kesey, who became a cultural icon of the counter-culture movement, was introduced to LSD.

In 1967 the government decided to take a more direct approach to its experimentation. The CIA had Dr. Louis Jolyon West set up operations in San Francisco. In the largest secret government test of mass drugging of a population in history, over 10 million hits of government produced LSD were dumped on the unsuspecting Haight Ashbury community.

Most of the government's clandestine drug experimentation programs were phased out by late 1967 but some projects were continued until 1973 when the new director of the CIA, James R. Schlesinger canceled a large number of questionable operations. The most interesting thing to me is that, in the government's attempt to find a way to control the minds of 'the people', it inadvertently empowered and spread the message of an already existing group of freethinking philosophers, poets, artists, musicians and every day people that were totally beyond their control. Essentially transforming what would've normally been considered a fringe element of society and placing them on the world stage in a position that enabled them to affect cultural norms on a global scale.

"Be Prepared" is the motto of the BSA or Boy Scouts of America and it's a pretty sound piece of advice. Unfortunately having never been a Boy Scout the significance has at times been completely lost on me. Take for instance the way I arrived in San Francisco. Having grown up for the most part in a desert climate, the idea of having to wear warm clothing during the summer months was something that just never occurred to me. In the desert it rarely got below 80° at night and during the daytime it was not uncommon to see it reach 110°. So when I showed up in the Bay

Area barefooted wearing only a T-shirt and Levi's it was pretty obvious that I had no idea what I was getting into.

On the way I met up with a couple guys who were heading to Oregon. We hitched a ride up to Santa Barbara, where we hopped a freight train heading north. When I hopped off the train near Watsonville it was so foggy that it was actually hard to see my own feet. Needless to say it was impossible to hitchhike in conditions like that so I stayed pretty far off the side of the road to minimize the possibility of getting hit by any passing vehicles. By the time the fog lifted I was so wet and cold that I was shaking uncontrollably.

I was eventually picked up by a very nice black gentleman driving a pickup who happened to be a retired police officer turned rancher. He said he could take me as far as Oakland but for some reason took pity on me and drove me all the way up to the corner of Haight and Masonic. He handed me an old horse blanket he had in the back of a truck and told me to be careful and wished me luck.

Compared to the sundrenched wide open desert spaces of Nevada and Southern California, San Francisco seemed like another planet. In Vegas a normal family dwelling was a single story unit with a front and back yard. In the Haight the average dwelling was a three story Victorian, the sides of which touched the buildings on either side of it with no yard whatsoever. It was cold, windy and overcast and not what I expected at all.

The first thing that struck me about the place was just how many freaks were on the street. The place was packed! There was so much going on. So many different scenes and clicks everywhere. It seemed more like a carnival midway than a city street. On one side of the street there was a group of Hare Krishnas dancing and chanting. On the other two uniformed policemen were busting a drug dealer who had a large baggie of pink tablets. The taller of the two cops held the guy by the back of his collar with one hand and held the bag of tablets high over his head and proceeded to announce to everybody on the street "take a good look at this guy, this is the guy that's been burning you, this is the guy that's been ripping you off". He then shoved the guy away from him, ripped open the baggie and threw all the pills out in the middle of the street. Then both of the officers got back in their car and drove away leaving the bewildered suspected drug dealer behind. Well, they certainly do things differently here than they do in Las Vegas, I thought.

Down the street there was a mixed group of Hells Angels and Gypsy Jokers hanging out in front of Love Burgers. Love Burgers was a little outside burger stand that took up the front part of an old bar called the Pall Mall. On the corner of Haight and Clayton was the Haight-Ashbury free medical clinic with its newly opened detox unit a few doors down across the street on Clayton. About half the block towards the park from the corner of Clayton and Haight Street, was the small local grocery store the locals called Mama Sans and Poppa Sans.

But at the moment the most interesting place was the fish and chips shop that was about two blocks farther up on the same side of the street. For twenty-five cents you'd get a large English style hand folded newspaper bag full of chips. For an additional quarter, they would throw in three large pieces of fish which you would then smother with malt vinegar. It was enough food to hold you for the rest of the day.

Due to the fact that I didn't know anybody, I wasn't sure how to go about finding a place to stay for the night. I had heard that the Diggers had a list of places for people to stay but by the time I found it all the places were filled up. By about 10 o'clock that night I had pretty much given up on trying to find a place to sleep indoors and started to look for any place I could curl up and go to sleep when I was approached by two Hells Angels. One of them asked me if I had a place to stay. When I said that I didn't he told me to come with him and that he'd take me to a place where I could crash for the night. We walked down the street to where he and the other Angels had their bikes parked in front of Love Burgers.

When the guys fired up their bikes I was told to get on the back of one and off we flew.

I can't tell you how fucking scared I was. I had no idea where I was going or what was going to happen when I got there. From all the horror stories I'd heard about the Hells Angels I figured I'd be lucky if I was still breathing in the morning. I thought I'd end up at some clubhouse being used as a target for knife throwing practice or something equally as unpleasant.

We pulled up to his house and both got off the bike. The guys said goodbye to each other and they all took off... except for the one Angel that asked me if I needed a place to stay. I don't know what I was expecting when I got inside but it certainly wasn't what I thought it might be.

Inside was a very normal house with the man's very normal girl-friend, a couple of other people and a nice bed for me to sleep in. As it turned out the man's name was Pete and he was the president of the San Francisco chapter of the Hells Angels. They were such kind, caring people that I had an incredibly hard time rectifying the image that everyone had of them. They fed me and gave me a place to sleep. Pete told me that I was welcome to stay there for a few days until I found a place.

The next morning we all had breakfast together and I got dropped off on Haight Street where I immediately set about trying to find a more permanent place to crash. That evening I once again found myself with Pete and his friends.

As it turned out it was a situation that was to continue for a few more days.

When I finally did find another place to stay it happened more by divine providence than any action on my part. I'd been walking up and down Haight Street all day, not having much luck, when I finally decided that I'd go up to Hippie Hill.

Just before I got to the park I ran into a kid that was selling acid for a dollar hit. We walked around the corner and when I handed him a dollar he pulled out a very large baggie and handed me four tabs. He said "give them to a couple of people and if they like it, tell them where they can find me".

I walked into the park and sat down to watch the drumming and dancing. Shortly afterwards a group of horse-mounted police officers showed up and started checking everyone's IDs. Not wanting to get caught with the LSD on me, and having no time to throw them away, I popped all 4 tablets into my mouth and swallowed them. After the officers had checked everyone out and decided to leave I asked one of the guys standing around if he knew anything about the type of acid that I'd just taken. When I described what they looked like to him his eyes got really big and he started laughing. He told me that they were four-way hits of the strongest stuff that was available and that I just taken more LSD that anyone he'd ever seen in his life and walked away shaking his head. Needless to say I don't remember much of what happened for the next several hours.

When I finally came down enough to recognize my immediate surroundings, I was on a couch in a beautiful Victorian flat at 1812 Scott Street. As I found out later, the people who lived there had found me wandering around the park in a less than coherent state and decided to get me off the streets before I got into any real trouble.

The guy's name was Vince Accetto. His girlfriend Kathy was a 5 foot tall green eyed mulatto girl with hair down to her waist. Maybe it was just the immediate after effects of the acid but I thought she was the most beautiful girl that I'd ever seen in my life. Turns out the acid had nothing to do with it. I still felt that way two months later.

Two or three days after I got there I was offered a room in the flat that was being vacated by Vince's brother Anthony. Not wanting to wear out my welcome with Angel Pete I took them up on the offer. Besides, I'd' had a fairly steady source of income ever since I'd been approached by a mendicant social worker who took me down to her office and signed me up for general assistance. This meant I could actually pay the rent!

Shortly after moving in I was introduced to our next-door neighbors, Tom and Rachel Donahue. Tom and his wife Rachel were both DJs at radio station KSAN. Tom's nickname was "Big Daddy." He'd started his radio career in 1949 at WTIP in West Virginia and continued at WIBG Philadelphia and finally WINX in Maryland. He moved to San Francisco in 1961. Upon his arrival he worked as a disc jockey on the AM radio station KYA and started his own record label called Autumn Records. He discovered, produced, recorded, and managed the Beau Brummels, a band considered to be the forerunner of all the San Francisco bands at that time.

In 1967 he revamped the foreign language FM station KMPX into what is considered to be America's first alternative freeform radio station, being the first man to introduce FM radio to rock 'n roll. Tom was the fi rst DJ to play noncommercial music by album oriented rock bands. After a pay strike on behalf of all the disc jockeys at KMPX went unresolved, Tom and Rachel moved on to radio station KSAN.

Like everyone else in the neighborhood, I listened to Tom's show almost every evening. When a band put out a new album you could be sure that Tom would be the first to have it and the first to play it from the first track to the last.

Tom's show was also one of the best ways to find out just what was going on in town. What events were happening and what bands were playing and where. Through a series of events that are still a bit hazy (it was the 60s after all) I met Chet Helms and Gary Scanlan at the Avalon Ballroom where I soon found myself falling into the role of a sometime paid volunteer moving band equipment and occasionally taking tickets at the door. It was during my time here that I reconnected with many of the people that I had met at the Newport Pop Festival such as Billy 'Kid' Candelerio, Bobby Weir and his girl friend Frankie who I took to hanging out with quite a bit.

One guy in particular that I became good friends with was Collin, a roadie that worked for Big Brother and the Holding Company. It was through him that I ended up working for the band during the last few gigs that Janis Joplin did with them. My limited personal experiences with Janis weren't the best to say the least. Knowing now how nervous and insecure she was back then it's not surprising that she always seemed grumpy and drank a lot, particularly so just before a gig. From the few interactions I had with her, I must say that I was much more enamored with her as a singer than I was with her as a person. Of course we all have bad days, and I was very young and impressionable. My opinion did eventually change, however, as I got know her better shortly before she passed away.

Because of the late hours that we kept at the Avalon it was sometimes easier for me to stay with Gary Scanlan and his girlfriend Cheryl at night on their houseboat in Sausalito. The houseboat, which I believe was called the Alpha, was right next to a large ferry boat named the Vallejo that was owned by the artist Jean Varda and British philosopher, writer, lecturer and interpreter of Eastern Philosophy Alan Watts.

Chet Helms with Gary Scanlan
Photo Credit - Joanne Fradkin

Alan had been a huge hero of mine ever since I had read his book "The Way of Zen" when I was in seventh grade. So coming face to face with him was more than a little daunting. I was so nervous when I met him that I honestly could barely speak - a situation he seemed to find quite amusing. This dynamic continued between us for a while, with him seeming to take great delight in watching how flustered I got every time he said good morning or hello to me. Fortunately I was able to overcome my nervousness enough to attend a couple of the talks that he gave on his houseboat. Unfortunately, however, I was in such an overtly altered state of consciousness when I did attend; that I can barely remember anything about it. Maybe Robin Williams was right when he said "if you remember the 60s, you weren't there."

For the most part though if I wasn't in the Sausalito I could be found hanging out in the Haight which is where all the action was during the daytime. The old Timothy Leary credo of: 'Turn on, Tune in and Drop out' was no longer applicable to the neighborhood's new arrivals. The daily mantra of the burgeoning teenage population in the neighborhood was now: 'Get food, Get laid & Get high'. Not necessarily in that order.

Gate 5 house boats 1968
Photo Credit - S.F. Oracle

During one of my quests for adventure I inadvertently ran afoul a shady group of so-called, street bikers. These were guys that looked like bikers and acted like bikers, but as far as anyone could tell had never actually ever been on a motorcycle. These guys were kind of an enigma in the neighborhood. They kept to themselves and basically refused to talk to anyone in the area. The basic consensus was that they were posers and phonies but no one was willing to tell them that to their faces. They hung out at a completely blacked out storefront up near Belvedere that fronted on Haight Street. If my memory serves me right (and it may not) the place was referred to as the Alpha Omega.

One evening I was accosted by two of the guys that hung out at the place who menacingly directed me into a small 10X10 room that contained no windows, a small bathroom off to the side, a dirty mattress and a large glass candle sitting in the middle of the floor. These guys then proceeded to inject me with speed at periodic intervals over the next few days, never once allowing me to leave or fall asleep the entire time.

The room was kept completely dark the entire time except for one lit candle and I had no idea what time it was or what day it was. From time to time I was brought food and water but after the first couple days I found that I was unable to eat anything at all.

The mental condition that results from enforced lack of sleep has got to be one of the most excruciating experiences that anyone can go through. It produces a profound sense of depression and delusional paranoia bordering on psychosis.

I was finally released when a couple of the guys in the neighborhood were tipped off that the kids being brought into the place were not coming back out and they decided to break in early one morning to see just what the hell was going on. As it turned out there were several of us locked in there and we had all been subject to the same treatment. The guys who had been doing this to us vanished shortly before the break-in, never to return.

I always wondered if the person who tipped the guys off to what was going on, and suggested that they go in there and get us out, was one of the people involved.

If this episode seems bizarre to you, imagine how it has seemed to me after all these years. I mean, why in the hell would anyone do something like this? Were they a group of sadistic psychopaths that were hanging around the neighborhood just waiting for a chance to pounce on a few unsuspecting kids? If so, why did they wait months before making any sort of a move? Or was something else going on.

Years later when I was having a conversation about the sixties with an ex Hells Angel I brought up the incident and asked him if he was familiar with that particular group of guys. He told me that yes indeed he was very familiar with them and that the Angels had been very interested in who they were back then. He told me that they had been government operatives conducting an investigation into the anti war movement using mind control experiments and were from the CIA.

Being a naturally skeptical person I decided to do a bit of research and did indeed find out that at the time the CIA was involved in a joint effort involving Military Intelligence, the FBI and local police departments in the Haight-Ashbury called: 'Operation Chaos' which was the code name for a domestic espionage project conducted by the Central Intelligence Agency. Now, whether this particular incident was actually part of that operation, no one can really say for sure, but it certainly does give you something to think about.

Chapter 14

Terrell, the leader of the Haight Street rescue party was a handsome twenty something African-American guy wearing a buckskin vest, Levi's and moccasins. He took a couple of us to an apartment building around the corner on Belvedere, where we were allowed to get cleaned up and crash out for a while. The next morning he told us that he thought it would be best if we got out of the neighborhood in case the kidnappers came back and decided they wanted to have another go at us. I was still so out of it from days of lack of sleep that I couldn't remember exactly where I lived and couldn't think of any place that I could go. He thought for a minute and then smiled and said "I've got the perfect place". He loaded me and my girlfriend - who had somehow managed to find me that night - into a van and took us out to a beautiful place way out in Marin County, called Rancho Olompali (aka the Grateful Dead Ranch).

The official story of the ranch goes something like this:

The ranch is located 3 miles north of Novato in Marin County. The name Olompali comes from the Miwok language and may be translated as 'southern village' or 'southern people'. The coastal Miwok inhabited at least one site within the area of the ranch continuously from as early as 6000 BC, until the early 1850s. In 1834 the ranch was part of an 8,887 acre Mexican land grant that was presented to Camilo Ynitia, the son of a Miwok chief, by Gov. Manuel Micheltorena. The ranch is the site of the oldest house built north of the San Francisco Bay. The Adobe brick structure was built in 1776 by the chief of the Olompali tribe. On June 24, 1846 the house became the site of The Battle of Olompali during the Bear Flag Revolt. The battle occurred when a skirmish broke out between a group of American bear flag-gers from Sonoma led by Henry Ford (who had days earlier declared California to be an independent republic), and a Mexican force of 50 men from Monterey, under the command of Col. Joaquin de la Torre met up at the house of Camilo Ynitia. In 1852, Ynitia sold most of the land to James Black of Marin with Ynitia retaining 1480 acres for himself. In 1863 the land passed from James Black to his daughter Mary Burdell, whose son James transformed the ranch into a country estate, building a 26 room mansion with formal Victorian style that incorporated the foundations in rooms of Ynitia's adobe house. The land and estate was eventually sold to Court Harrington who in turn sold it to the University of San Francisco to be used as a Jesuit retreat. In the 1960s the University of San Francisco sold the Rancho several times, each time the buyers defaulted and the property reverted back to the University. The Ranch's most famous tenant was the Grateful Dead. During the Dead's brief stay, the ranch became a gathering place for San Francisco rock musicians. In 1967 Don McCoy leased the ranch and turned it into a utopian communal living Center.

So much for history...

The place was beautiful, far beyond my imagination. Having grown up in a desert climate, I found it almost unbelievable that any place could be so green. The ranch was nestled in the beautiful rolling, tree covered hills of northern California. The beautiful main house had over 20 rooms in it and scattered around the area were several other outbuildings, which included a very large barn and a fairly good-sized completely insulated and paneled miniature children's playhouse. The ranch also had an Olympic sized swimming pool and a very beautiful large organic garden.

We were brought into the kitchen and offered soup and home-made bread which we ate while Terrell told the 'family' members our story and why he had brought us there. After bit of discussion it was decided that we would be allowed to stay, but that we would have to do something to earn our keep. I quickly volunteered my monthly government allowance and was told that would do nicely.

The next problem was finding a place to put us up. Initially we were installed in the kids playhouse which, while too small to stand up in, was big enough to house a king-size mattress with a little bit of floor space left over. It was clean, had real glass windows with curtains, a locking door and electricity. I loved it! It was sort of an Alice in Wonderland experience.

Much of my first couple weeks at the ranch are pretty hazy because I will still recovering from my enforced confinement back in the Haight. One night shortly after my arrival, I was surprised to run into Billy 'Kid' Candelario down by the main house. We greeted each other and he asked me what I was doing there. I told him what happened in the Haight and how I was brought to the ranch. I then asked him what he was doing there. He told me that he and a couple of the Grateful Dead crew guys had been living there since the days that the Dead had the place, a year or so before. For me this was great news because it meant that I had somebody that was closer to my own age (both of us still in our teens) that was involved on the music side of things to hang out with. The only other person on the ranch that was close to my age, besides my soon-to-be ex-girlfriend, was a very nice girl named Noelle Barton. Everyone else was either in their late 20s to middle 40s or children under the age of 12.

While everyone was nice to me, I never felt like I actually fit in very well. I was pretty relieved when Bobby Weir and Frankie dropped by and took me over to their place that they shared with Pigpen to stay for a while. The timing for this was absolutely perfect. I desperately needed to get away from my supposed girlfriend who had recently taken to sleeping with anyone, anywhere, anytime at the ranch. Not only was it emotionally painful, it was turning out to be quite embarrassing. The guys were always asking me where she was and most of the women wanted to know if she was gone yet.

After several failed attempts to get her to either stop fucking around or leave, I jumped at the first chance to remove myself from the situation. She was soon off the ranch and shortly after that, out of my life. At least for a while…

Bob, Pigpen and Frankie were sharing a duplex somewhere in the San Rafael, San Anselmo, Corte Madera area (once again the memory fails). Pigpen had one apartment in the duplex and Bob and Frankie had the one on the other side. It was a pretty cool situation, though in truth I had always felt a bit on edge around Pigpen. This was mostly because the first time I ever met him he ended up shouting at me.

The story goes something like this: one night after a gig, we were all hanging around the backstage area and as usual there was a joint being passed around. Not being a big fan of the stuff myself, I attempted to pass it off to the nearest person to me when it came my way. Unfortunately that person was Pigpen, who rather than saying no thanks yelled: "Don't hand me that fucking hippie shit!" Bob said "don't worry about it he always acts like that around drugs". He didn't take them and certainly didn't like them. He eventually became a lot friendlier toward me when he found out later that I didn't smoke that hippie shit either. None of us did for that matter, not Bobby, Frankie, me or Pig.

One of my final flings with the demon weed came one day when Jack Cassidy (bass player for the Jefferson airplane) picked me up while I was hitchhiking back to the Haight from the Avalon. Jack, as usual, was driving his trusty old Citroen. After we got a few blocks he nodded towards the glove compartment and had me take out a small tin Sucrets box that had a couple joints in it. Not wanting to seem snooty or ungrateful, I accepted the lit joint when he passed it to me and began casually smoking away on it. I had always been a lightweight when it came to weed, so I should have suspected that if Jack had some, it was probably strong enough to be radio-active.

By the time he dropped me off at Haight and Masonic I was completely unable to speak and so dizzy that he had to help me out of the car. I gave him a halfhearted wave as he drove off, walked around the corner and threw up all over the side of the building. As far as I was concerned that was the end of that. I haven't smoked weed since…

While things were relaxed at the duplex, we also seemed to be constantly on the move. Bob and Jerry had a side project called 'Bobby Ace and the Cards from the Bottom of the Deck' (the project eventually morphed into the New Riders of the Purple Sage) and of course the Dead always seemed to be playing somewhere.

After one particularly hectic day of running around, Bob, Frankie and I showed up for a gig at the Fillmore West. Having not eaten all day we found ourselves confronted with 30 or so tinfoil lined Styrofoam coolers each stacked to the top with delicious smelling, piping hot chocolate chip cookies. We were dying of hunger and they smelled so good, but one of the first things you learn from being around the Dead is that you never eat or drink anything anybody hands to you.

About that time one of the crew guys walked in and told us not to touch anything because Bear (Owsley) had been hard at work on those cookies. But, he said that Betty had kept a couple of containers back that were safe to eat. He showed us where they were and Bob, Frankie, Jerry and I started chowing down on them like there was no tomorrow. About 5 min. later he came tearing back in white as a sheet and told us that he had made a mistake and that those were bear's special cookies and that the safe ones were in the other dressing room. We had all eaten somewhere between five and 10 cookies each and we all knew very clearly that we were basically fucked!

How the guys got through the set that night I'll never know. Frankie and I were so fucked up that I don't think either of us left the backstage area till well after the gig was over. We weren't sure how we were going to get back to the house so we hung around the club as long as we could until Smitty, the security guard at the Fillmore, told us he had to lock the place up and go home.

By this time Jerry thought that he was in good enough shape to drive so we all got in his car and prepared for the trip home. Jerry put his key in the ignition, started the car, put it in gear and drove straight into the back of a car parked in front of us. It was hilarious, though I'm pretty sure I didn't think so at the time. Jerry turned off the car and sat there in the front seat shaking his head repeating over and over, Fuck man! Fuck man! We all got out of the car and started wandering around trying to figure out how the hell we were going to get home and I somehow got separated from everybody.

At some point in my addled brained state I decided to hitchhike back to the house. Unfortunately I got confused and ended up hitchhiking towards Berkeley instead of Marin County which is in the opposite direction. The next thing I knew I was on the Bay Bridge, peaking on acid, and the guy driving the car that just picked me up put his hand on my leg.

It's at this point that I realised that things weren't going quite as well as I had hoped they would. After a few moments of mind numbing confusion, I removed the guy's hand and told him to let off at the first place he can. Unfortunately, that place turns out to be Berkeley, which because of the ongoing series of Vietnam War protests, has lately come to resemble an armed camp more than a college town. I've got to tell you, you haven't lived until you've tried dodging the TAC squad stoned out of your mind on acid at four in the morning.

I finally made it back to the ranch to find that not only was my girlfriend (thankfully) gone, but so was my spot in the Playhouse. This turned out to be not much of an issue because one of the guys that had been living in the barn had recently relocated to one of the other houses and the loft was now available.

The loft was a lot less cozy than Playhouse had been, but it was a hell of a lot bigger and potentially a lot more dangerous if you aren't paying attention. Essentially the loft was the upper part of a closed in set of horse stalls that had originally been used as a hayloft. The rear and right side of the loft buttied up against the rear and side of the barn. The other two edges were open to the main barn area with about a 12 foot drop to the floor. To get to the loft you had to climb a very old, very sturdy ladder that was attached to the side of it. The area was fairly good-sized - about 15' x 20' with plenty of headroom. In it I put a queen sized bed, a small table with two chairs and a lamp, a chest of drawers and a large Indian throw rug that covered most of area.

I shared the barn with a two other guys. One, a black haired guy in his mid-30s - a devotee of Gurdjieff - lived directly below me with this dog. The other guy, who occupies the barn with us, was bizarre beyond belief. He was a six foot seven triple Leo, with a perfect physique, extremely long blonde hair and a Col. Sanders type mustache and goatee with long sideburns. He wore small round wire-rimmed glasses and no clothing whatsoever. I honestly can't think of a single time that I ever saw him wear clothes.

Besides being incredibly fond of himself, he had an absolutely delusional belief in his own abilities. This bizarre behavior of his manifested itself one day when the Grateful Dead were playing at the ranch and he decided that he is going to go up on stage and show Jerry how to play guitar. The delusional aspect of this whole charade was that the guy had never played guitar before in his life! I honestly don't think he'd ever even picked one up. It would have been comical, if the guy hadn't been so goddamned annoying. As I came to learn firsthand, this guy, whose name was Stephen, was always doing something like this, and it was because of this strange behavior of his that he became the inspiration for the Grateful Dead song 'St. Stephen'...

Even though the band was no longer living at the ranch they still maintained a very strong presence there and Olompali was considered to be the place where the Grateful Dead's extended family members lived. As a result of this we were the first ones to have a chance to try out all the newest batches of LSD that Bear/ Owsley made before they were ever released to the public. Needless to say it was always of the highest quality.

Unfortunately, however, it was because of that I had come to unquestioningly trust the LSD that we were receiving, that I found myself lying in a hospital bed in Greenbrae, California. It seems that someone had decided to drop off a batch of small glass vials containing a purple liquid that turned out to be an extremely concentrated form of liquid PCP at the ranch, without bothering to tell anybody what it was. The problem was that it looked exactly like the liquid purple Owsley I had taken years before and that stuff was legendary! As far as I and many other people were concerned it was the best LSD ever made.

The minute I emptied the contents of the vial into my mouth, however, I knew something was wrong. It had a sort of a bitter taste to it. Liquid LSD doesn't have any kind of a taste of all. About 20 minutes after taking it was when the real nightmare began.

I was walking from the barn down the road to the main house, when I had the bizarrely unaccountable sensation of watching the road slowly tilt up and smack me on the side of my head. "That's weird" I thought to myself "I'm still standing straight up. Why is it doing that?" I tried pushing it away from me but it just wouldn't budge. The next thing I knew there were several people standing around me and for some unknown reason I couldn't remember how to breathe. Someone picked me up and told me to relax and I continued to not remember how to breathe until I finally passed out. I came to a short time later and once more totally fail to remember how to breathe until I pass out again. Three days later I was released from Marin County General Hospital, feeling like I'd been run over by a semi with no memory of the event what so ever...

Because of the ranch's open-door policy, there was always a steady stream of visitors coming and going at will. So I was pleasantly surprised one day to find that one of the visitors was an old friend of mine from Los Angeles Robbie Robison - who played guitar with the band Clear Light. I had originally met Robbie in Las Vegas when his band played the Teen Beat club a couple years before. I asked him what he'd been up to and he said that he was just passing through on his way to Oregon. It turned out that he had come to the ranch in the company of couple of guys from the city, crazy Arthur and English David, who were Avalon regulars. I told Robbie he was welcome to stay with me until he was ready to hit the road, and he readily accepted my offer. Robbie and I sat down to play guitars and shoot to shit, while Arthur and David wandered off to explore the ranch. Just before dark as they were leaving, the boys stopped by and invited us down to their house in San Francisco at 83 Noe Street.

Olompali early days
Photo Credit - State archives

Chapter 15

After living the rustic country style life at the ranch as well as crashing around the city in places that were for the most part seedy at best, I was totally unprepared for the Noe Street house. It was a typical Victorian style flat that seemed somehow untouched by the ravages of time. While the outside showed slight signs of weathering, the inside still retained much of the original style furnishings and architectural nuances from the height of the Victorian era. The wood paneling and scrolled arch doorways were still in pristine condition and many of the walls were hung with Victorian era hand-woven tapestries, with the halls being hung with thick purple velvet draperies, floor to ceiling. The house's original gas lighting system, while seldom used, was still fully functional. The beautiful overhead hand cut glass chandeliers in each of the bedrooms were still in place and in perfect condition. It was hard to believe that people lived in such beautifully built and furnished homes over 100 years before, and harder still to believe that any of it was able to survive the plasticizing ravages of the 1950s.

The house itself was presided over by Paula, a thin willowy creature reminiscent of a silent era film star. She shared the house with her ex husband - turned personal manservant - Arthur, Janice Joplin's part time girlfriend Patty Cakes, their other roommate Puanani and her baby daughter Nika and a beautiful redhead named Fayette Hauser who had recently arrived from Colorado with Nancy Gurley.

It was during one of my many visits to this house that I was introduced to an amazing young lady who was to become my dearest and closest friend. A young woman with an infectious smile and a wild mane of long curly blonde hair. She wore large hoop earrings, bracelets that covered both arms all the way to her elbows, scarves, peasant blouses and dark bell sleeved mid-length sorceress jackets. It was no wonder that she was known as Gypsy Joanne (Joanne Fradkin).

Joanne had originally come to the city to attend San Francisco State, but she, like her classmate and friend George Hunter (founding member of the Charlatans) before her, had decided to forgo her formal education in order to pursue a more artistic bohemian life-style. This led her to become a highly respected and sought after member of the lightshow community, working with such light-show pioneers as Bill Hamm, Glenn McKay, Jerry Abrams and the Brotherhood of Light.

Joanne lived in the notorious Russian embassy building with James and Nancy Gurley, Martoon (the Family Dog's resident alchemist magician) and several other Family Dog members. The building's real name was the Westerfield house. It had originally been constructed in 1889 for local banker and candy baron, William Westerfield. It earned the nickname - the Russian embassy - decades later when a group of czarist Russians ran a social club out of it.

In 1965 the house was occupied by a group calling itself the Calliope company, San Francisco's first hippie commune. In 1966 the house was rented to Los Angeles underground filmmaker Kenneth Anger, an avant-garde little gay man who made short fetishistic styled films. Like some California visionaries of the time, Anger was drawn to the dark side and had a lifelong obsession with Alastair Crowley, Britain's notorious sex magician and self-professed beast, who had left his footprint on the Los Angeles community of Anger's youth. By 1968 the house was occupied by Joanne and several other people including the members of the Family Dog who promoted the shows and ran the Avalon ballroom.

Martoon in the tower room of the Russian Embassy
Photo Credit - S.F. Archives

Meanwhile, back at the ranch...

Ranch life was idyllic beyond compare but I still didn't feel like I fit in there. While I regularly contributed funds I still felt like I needed to do a bit more. So throwing caution to the wind I presented myself to the head gardener Peter and boldly volunteered myself for service in the garden. This, as it turned out, was something that I was absolutely not cut out for. I had no affinity and no skill for gardening whatsoever. Far from having a green thumb, I seemed to have 10 of them and they were all black. Hell, I could wilt a zucchini plant at 10 paces just by looking at it. Not a very useful superpower I must admit, but if the X-Men ever needed someone who could wreak havoc on an organic garden, I'm their guy!

After giving up the whole notion of gardening as a bad job, I next presented myself at the bakery. If Olompali was famous for anything besides the Grateful Dead and naked hippies, it was the massive amount of bread that they baked and shared with other communes. It soon, however, became very apparent that a 16-year-old boy had no business being in a kitchen run by very competent and very dedicated women bakers. While they were grateful for the offer of help, it soon became apparent that I was more in the way than anything else.

Around this same time my friend Robert returned to the ranch with an absolutely beautiful tipi that he picked up on his last visit to the rez. Robert, who was Lakota, had been one of our regular residents though he had recently taken to traveling between the ranch, South Dakota and the Four Corners area quite a bit lately. He also brought back with him a very large sack full of the fi rst peyote buttons that I'd ever seen.

Robert and I had been running buddies ever since we first met and I was really glad to see him. We took off scouting around looking for the perfect place to set up the tipi and eventually settled on an old Miwok campsite close to the northern edge of the ranch.

After getting Robert settled in I decided to try to bum a ride into Novato to pick up some tobacco.

On the way down from the tipi to the main housing area, I ran into Terry, a young guy from Petaluma who looked after the horses there on the ranch. Terry had recently come into possession of an old 1957 Panhead that had belonged to a member of one of the bike clubs that had recently been killed riding a small off-road motorcycle.

I told him I was trying to get into town and he said that he needed to go in as well and that I could ride in with him on the bike if I wanted. It turned out to be one of the worst experiences I've ever had on a motorcycle in my life. A total fucking nightmare. Not only did the bike not have a passenger seat, it also didn't have any passenger pegs. I don't know what the hell I'd been thinking when I accepted his offer.

I soon found myself vibrating off the back of a speeding motorcycle going nearly 90 miles an hour with my right pant leg on fire from contact with the exhaust pipe and screaming at the top of my lungs in a vain attempt to get Terry to stop the bike!

By the time I got his attention I was sitting on the taillight bracket with both feet dragging on the ground and my hands bleeding from trying to hold onto the rear fender. I was so scared that I was white as a ghost and nearly threw up when we finally got stopped.

It was right about then that it became crystal clear to me that I really didn't need the tobacco that bad and I decided to hitchhike back to the ranch...

Up north at the Morning Star commune, Lou Gottlieb, the owner, was having trouble with the law again. Lou had been waging a losing legal battle with irate neighbors and local officials in an attempt to keep the ranch's open land policy going. However, problems of a different sort had been dogging the community for quite a while.

Because the community was opened to everyone, some of the people who began showing up were more along the lines of violent alcoholic speed freaks than peace loving hippies. With mass arrests taking place at the commune and daily confrontations with local police authorities escalating, Don McCoy the owner of Olompoli - a close friend of MorningStar owner Lou Gottlieb - invited the members of the MorningStar community to come down and stay at the ranch.

If I had to pick the perfect cliché to describe the situation it would be " going to hell in a handbasket" because that's what it felt like a few days after we were inundated by the influx of people showing up at the ranch from up north.

In just a few short days the ranch had gone from being a sparsely populated idyllic LSD fueled Wonderland, to an overcrowded tent city for alcoholic speed freak winos.

Don't get me wrong, the longtime residents of MorningStar were for the most part very good people, but the people that had been attracted there as of late were nowhere near the caliber of people the original residents were. Unfortunately the vast majority of the people who showed up seemed to fall into that category.

Wishing to avoid the general chaos that was now taking place around the Main building areas, I gathered my few belongings from my loft in the barn and headed up to the tipi to hang out with Robert for a while.

Fortunately within a few days the ranch was pretty much back to normal with most of the visitors heading up north to Bill Wheeler's ranch which he'd opened up to all the MorningStar residents. For me however things began to change rapidly. My old girlfriend showed back up at the ranch, which made things uncomfortable as hell. Chester found a new place to open the Family Dog that needed to be made ready and I wanted to spend more time with Joanne. Thus I found myself spending less and less time at the ranch and more and more time in the city.

I found Joanne staying at the Noe Street house, having just moved from the Russian embassy which had been sold to a new owner. She told me she had found a really great basement apartment over on Fell Street which was directly right across the Panhandle from the house that James and Nancy Gurley and Richard Hudgins were sharing at 1965 Oak St. It should be ready to move into in a few days she said.

I asked her what she had been up to since I'd last seen her and she told me that she had been working pretty steadily with Jerry Abrams Headlights and that she was working that night at the Avalon. She asked if I cared to tag along. The truth of the matter was that if she had asked me to accompany her to be burned at the stake I would've readily accepted because I had such a mad crush on her. So since I was planning to be there to help Gary out anyway I readily accepted her offer…

It's at about this point in the story that things start to get a little bit more disjointed than they already have been. So much was going on at that time that it's hard to keep linear track of any of it.

Here is a brief synopsis:

Joanne moved to the Fell Street house and I took over her room at 83 Noe.

Lady Paula - the Noe Street Acid Queen - had recently been released from the hospital after having broken her back in a freak car acci-dent up at Harbinger Hot Springs.

Because of her condition she needed help with the business and I found myself making up large quantities of blue blotter acid on a regular basis in an effort to help her out and make a little dough on the side.

Bill Graham had opened up the Fillmore West at the old Carousel Ballroom. It was open four nights a week starting with the Tuesday audition/jam night with regular show nights on Thursday, Friday and Saturday evenings.

Steve Gaskin held his Monday night class at the Straight Theater and of course there was the Avalon Ballroom as well. We all had someplace to go every night.

If I wasn't at the Avalon I was at the Fillmore. If I wasn't in the city I was up at the ranch. If I wasn't in either of those places I was in Sausalito or I was at Bob and Frankie's place.

Basically, I didn't have a care in the world. I was living life to the fullest and having one hell of a good time doing it, little realizing that things would soon get a whole lot weirder than I could possibly have imagined...

Chapter 16

660 The Great Hwy. was the address of the new location for the Family Dog or as it was officially known The Family Dog on the Great Highway.

I got my first glimpse of it in the middle of April 1969 when Joanne and I had come down to see if we could help with getting the place set up.

The building had originally been built as a dance hall in 1884 and had started out life as the Ocean Beach Pavilion. Sometime between the years of 1908 and 1915 the building served as the training camp of heavyweight boxing champion Jack Johnson. By 1929 the building had become a very popular chicken dinner house and nightclub called Topsy's Roost. In the early 1950s the building housed a dance hall called the Surf Club and by 1964 the building had been converted to a slot car racing track.

The inside of the high ceilinged building was dominated by a large rectangular dance floor that ran from north to south, parallel to the shoreline across the street. At the south end of the hall a stage was being built with electrical wiring and cables for the sound equipment already being run. The majority of the work involved cleaning up, patching up holes and painting. Most of the work was being done by volunteers consisting of various band members and people from the community as the venue was intended to be run more along the lines of a co-op then a traditional concert hall.

The official grand opening of The Family Dog on The Great High-way was June 13 - 15 with the Jefferson Airplane, the Charlatans and Devils Kitchen. In truth, the building had been hosting Stephen Gaskins Monday night class for some time by then.

About every six weeks a group get-together was held that was called the Meeting of the Common, or as we referred to it the Commons meetings. They involved artists from all different fields that had an interest in participating in the planning of how the venue was to be run for the next six weeks or so. This included members of the light show community, the spiritual community, the theater community and of course the musical community.

These gatherings had a tendency to resemble more of a sponta-neous good-natured free-for-all than an actual organized meeting. Most of the participants seemed to view the meetings as the perfect opportunity to bring the entire family with them for a day at the beach. The place was usually filled with dogs and children running wild through the building while the grownups took the opportu-nity to catch up with each other and conduct a little business at the same time.

The impending weirdness that I mentioned earlier started off like this: one evening my friend Claude Palmer and I were at the Family Dog on the beach shortly after it first opened. The first band had just finished. It was in between sets and we were listening to another fellow who was telling us about something called the Book of Urantia when this guy walks up to me and says "You know, there are beings that exist in the same time/space continuum as we do but they exist on a higher vibrational level. They have a physical existence but because it's on a higher vibrational plane we can't see them and *They'd like to speak to you if you're interested.*"

Family Dog Great Highway
Photo Credit - Unknown Polaroid

At first I looked at the guy like he was out of his fucking mind, but he said it so matter of factly that I thought, "what if, what if it's true?" So I said "sure, why not?" Just that lamely, "sure why not?" The guy nodded his head, smiled and walked away. I never saw him again. I didn't think too much of it really. In fact I pretty much forgot all about it until a couple weeks later when the most bizarre things started happening.

I was walking down Haight Street one afternoon when out of the corner of my eye I noticed this beautiful red Mustang convertible drive up beside me. As I turned my head to get a better look at it the driver said "get in, let's go". None of the usual 'hi how are you' or 'where you been' stuff just "get in, let's go." It was Robert my Lakota friend that I had lived in the tipi with up on the ranch during the summer. The whole incident seemed a bit odd from the beginning really. None of us back then ever had any money. Things like that weren't that important to us. So I was quite surprised and more than a bit confused to see him driving a car at all let alone such a nice one.

After receiving his initial refusal to tell me what was going on until we were on our way, I got in and he drove us to a very secluded house out in Muir woods in Marin County just north of San Francisco. Obviously, who ever owned the place had quite a bit of money tied up in it as it was quite large and very nicely furnished.

It felt kinda weird going into the house of someone I didn't know when they weren't home but Robert had a key to the place so I guessed it was okay. Right after we got inside he handed me some acid and went to make a couple phone calls. A few minutes later he came back and said "I've got to go take care of a couple things. Stay here. I'll be back a little bit later."

I took the acid and sat down to wait for him to come back, all the while feeling slightly uncomfortable because I was in someone's home.

Now I've taken a lot of psychedelics at very high doses so I know what to expect. Things began to unfold in the usual way at first. But... something very different began to happen this time, something new in the form of what I can only describe as a sort of a moving sound or signal. When I think about it the best analogy I can come up with is that it was like when you touch the screen of some laptop computers and you get a kind of fish-eye distortion where your finger comes into contact with the screen. This, however, was more on the level of the field of conscious awareness and it was moving around. At about the same time I got a very clear message on what I guess you could describe as the sub vocal level that was very clear and very distinctly telling me to "Pay Attention to the signal. Keep your focus on it no matter where it seems to move."

At first it was hard to do. I'd get distracted by an itch and I would be gently reminded to keep my focus on the signal. It took me awhile but I finally got it comfortably in focus. I was then told to expand my focus to take in the ceiling light a few feet in front of me. So I kept my focus on the signal and expanded my awareness to take in the ceiling light and the fucking thing blew up! Just like that! As soon as I looked at it! It shattered!

It startled the shit out of me and made me jerk around. In so doing I glanced at the TV across the room which had been on with the sound off. The second I looked at it, it fucking blew up as well! The television made a loud popping sound and a dark black streak appeared across the inside of the tube!

I can't even describe how freaked out I was. I just sat there going "What the Fuck? What the Fuck was that about?" The voice/message/whatever came back and said very clearly and with an air of amusement "You all have the ability to do this".

None of the other lights or electrical devices in the house were effected, just the light and the TV.

At that point all I wanted to do was get as far away from that house as fast as I possibly could. I mean, if the people who owned the house came back while I was still there, how in the hell was I supposed to explain to them what happened to their bloody TV and the damned overhead light. I can just hear the explanation now. "I'm dreadfully sorry. I had a sort of LSD fueled psychic freak out and telekinetically destroyed your television set by accident." It was an absurd thought. Hell, it was an absurd situation. One I didn't want to find myself in.

Fortunately the people didn't return home that night. Unfortunately, Robert didn't either. He didn't come back until the next day. When I woke up the next morning on the couch the light was still cracked and the TV still had a black burn mark across the inside of the tube.

I was so freaked out by the whole incident that I didn't know whether or not to mention anything about it to Robert. Rather than risk looking like the looneytune I already felt like, I decided to keep my mouth shut even though I had a strong suspicion that he knew more about what happened than I did…

Okay, what the hell was I supposed to do with that? Was it a pure straight forward hallucination? Judging by the condition of the light and TV that next morning it seemed highly unlikely. Coincidence? Well, in a normal 3 dimensional view of reality based on Cartesian rationalism it seemed the more likely scenario. Or possibly it had something to do with brain structure and the odd way it has of processing information. For some strange reason these explanations just didn't seem to serve the situation very well.

My natural inclination was to just write it off as a sort of psychic or mental anomaly. I would have too if it had stopped right then and there.

However...

Chapter 17

Things quickly got back to normal. Normal for San Francisco at that time period anyway. Joanne and I spent a lot of time traveling between her place on Fell Street, 83 Noe Street and the new Family Dog location. When I didn't have much going on Paula would put me to work mixing grams of pure crystal LSD in distilled water with a small amount of blue food coloring which I then applied to small square pieces of blotter paper with an eye dropper.

Joanne and I took to hanging out with James and Nancy Gurley whose house was right across the Panhandle from Joanne's place on Fell St.

Because I was so close by Nancy would sometimes have me come over and watch their son Hongo when she and James had to go out. I spent most of my babysitting time fooling around with one or another of James's many guitars. Upon his return one day James walked in and plugged the guitar I was playing into one of his amps. He then picked up one of the other guitars and without a word started jamming with me. I got so nervous during that first jam that I thought I might actually throw up. Hanging out and babysitting for one of your musical heroes is one thing but actually getting the chance to play music with them is quite another thing entirely.

Before long I was jamming with James and sometimes Sam Andrew at least once a week. During our first jam session with Sam, James decided that I would make a much better bass player than a guitar player. He explained to me that "guitar players were a dime a dozen" and because there were so many of them it was hard for them to get gigs. "But", he said, "everybody needs a bass player, so you are now a bass player" and that was that.

The next time I showed up at his house with my guitar he took it and put it in his closet and grabbed another case out of it and handed it to me. "Here, this is yours" he said. Inside the case was a red Gibson semi hollow body EB2 bass. I was so blown away that he would even think of doing something like that for me I was speechless. That one action changed my life and gave me a chance to have a great career - that is, if you happen to think being a starving musician is a great career. Thanks a lot James!

Sam and James
Photo Credit - S.F. Oracle

Not long after this I found myself in another extremely bizarre situation.

After spending most of the day making up blotter acid for Paula, Joanne and I decided to head down to the beach to attend Steve Gaskins Monday night class. I'm not sure exactly how or when it began, but sometime during the class I suddenly found myself floating in a timeless deep black space surrounded by extremely humorous disembodied voices and hundreds of clouds of light, each one a different color. Electric reds, blues, greens, purples, violet, orange and yellows, each one very much alive and very much aware. The cloud's main form of communication took place by passing through one another. During this process a complete and total exchange of experience and knowledge took place, each one coming away with the deepest memories of the other. The level of vulnerability and intimacy involved was so far beyond anything human beings could possibly imagine that words fail the situation. At the same time, the disembodied voices seemed to be involved in some sort of zany Marx brothers' type scenario. The most disconcerting part of it was that, while the situation was strange, it was also excruciatingly familiar at the same time. It felt almost like walking into your old childhood home for the first time in many, many years.

After what seemed like an eternity, I began to notice one sweet little voice in particular that seemed to be asking me a question. As I focused on the question I suddenly found myself lying on the floor in the center of a circle of a hundred or so chanting people and looking into the smiling face of a three-year-old boy who asked me "are you dead?" I laughed and told him "I think so." He then started giggling and ran off the find his mom.

Needless to say I had no idea why or how I ended up in the middle of that circle. All I knew was that I just wanted to get up, go to the bathroom, find Joanne and get the hell out of there as quickly as possible.

While this incident was not nearly as astonishing as the event that took place at the house in Muir Woods it was also not what

I considered a typical psychedelic experience. Yes there were the usual geometric patterns but no motion related trails and no feelings of introspective euphoria.

It was like being transported into a completely different world while still in possession of your full faculties. The most interesting aspect of it was that I remembered, very clearly, everything that occurred down to the minutest detail for several weeks afterward.

The only explanation I could come up with for what happened was that I had absorbed a not too insignificant amount of LSD while helping out Paula that day. Either that or I had finally managed to develop a case of self induced brain damage and was completely out of my mind. It was more likely a combination of the two. (another fine example of Better Living through Chemistry)!

Chapter 18

The basement of 1793 Fell St. looked more like the library of the 15th century alchemist Nicholas Flamel than someone's living quarters. Its walls were covered with shelves containing volume upon volume of obscure occult manuscripts in every known language. The ceilings were covered with Middle Eastern tapestries. The statuary that was scattered around the place was mostly of the early Egyptian dynastic style. The space near the ceiling just to the left of the front door was occupied by a stuffed three-foot African fruit bat named Bela. The back wall of the living room was entirely taken up by a large altar containing the following: Several antique crystal balls made of either glass or obsidian.

A large eye of Horus.

Seven or eight canisters of magical incense.

A large centrally placed Brass incense burner.

Three different types of Tarot decks.

A large array of tall glass prayer candles.

A twelve inch tall statue of Isis.

Several hand carved antique scarabs and a human skull.

On the floor the altar was flanked on either side by a three-foot tall statue of the Egyptian God Anubis.

Joanne shared this space with a sweet beautiful black Greyhound that was also named Anubis. Because Joanne acted as the unofficial host for the Family Dog, it was not uncommon to find any number of out-of-town musicians crashed out on the couch or the spare room just off the kitchen. You could always find someone like Dickie Peterson from the band Blue Cheer passed out on the couch or in a corner somewhere.

Shortly after I moved in we played host to the English group 'Manfred Mann' (Doo Wah Diddy, Blinded by the Light). It was these fine gentleman who introduced me to warm Guiness Stout and Indian food and set me off on my life long quest to find the ultimate dish of chicken vindaloo.

Joanne Fradkin 1980s
Photo Credit - Fayette Hauser

Because of my relocation to Fell Street, I found myself once again spending a lot of time in the Haight. Over the time period beginning in 1966 to 1969 the neighborhood had gone from being a haven for freethinking artistic bohemians to a playground for radical politicos, heroin dealers, speed freaks and rip-off artists of all shapes and colors.

Beginning in 1968 a concerted effort to "clean up the neighborhood" had been put in effect by Mayor Joe Alioto. He began his cleanup campaign by ordering random police sweeps by the San Francisco TAC squad on Haight Street while his wife Angela began to take full advantage of the falling property prices and bought up everything that she could get her hands on in the neighborhood.

By the fall of 1968 heroin was as readily available as LSD had been the previous year. It quickly began to take a heavy toll on the community.

My first encounter with the world of heroin came one day when Janice called James at the Oak Street house wanting to know if he had any dope. Her regular connection was out. He told her that he only had enough for the next couple days and that he too was going to be in the same position very shortly. Having overheard the phone conversation I told JamesI thought I knew where to find some. He informed Janice and she arrived at his house within the hour. She handed me $60 and I immediately headed for the hole in the wall pizza place on Haight Street to look for a young fancy dressed black kid named Delicious who hung out there.

I had first met the guy walking down Haight Street a couple of months earlier. I was just passing the pizza joint when he stepped out of the doorway and said "Hey man, are you lookin"? (Are you lookin' is drug dealer slang for 'are you looking to purchase any drugs'?)

I asked him what he had and he opened his mouth to show me several tightly wrapped brightly colored balloons. I stared at him with a puzzled look on my face. he said "You know, smack, boy, downtown". It took me a few seconds but fi nally I realized he was selling heroin. "Oh yeah, right" I said "uh not right now man, thanks though".

Ever since that first encounter I had run into him almost every time I'd passed the pizza joint with each of us exchanging greetings.

When I finally got to the pizza joint he was nowhere to be found. "Typical" I thought, "cops and drug dealers are all alike. There's never one around when you need them".

Seeing one of the guys that he regularly hung out with sitting inside the pizza joint I went in and asked if he knew where Delicious was. The guy just stared at me like I was a creature from outer space and acted like he didn't understand English.

Not getting any help there and not wanting to disappoint Janice, I decided to cruise the neighborhood looking for him. An hour later I had given up and was just heading back towards Oak Street when I finally ran into him and was able to cop six dime bags of Mexico's finest for the Queen of rock 'n roll.

Upon my triumphant return from my very successful venture I was kind of bummed out to find Janice more annoyed at the delay than thankful for the effort I put in trying to get some dope for her. Oh well, she was a dope sick drug addict after all.

The news of my success hit the local grapevine with astonishing speed. The result being that whenever any of Marin County's upper-crust rock 'n roll crowd got really stuck and were unable to find any dope they would eventually come looking for me. Over the next few months this happened quite a lot.

The very next morning someone arrived at Joanne's flat with a message for me saying that a gentleman who was good friends with Janice - and pretty much everyone else in the Northern California music scene - wanted to know if I was available to meet with him.

At about three that afternoon I was introduced to a guy in his early 30s, with fairly long curly ginger colored hair and a beard, named Roger. He was tall and thin and very well-dressed in a hip sort of way. He also had the clear eyed look of someone who didn't use hard drugs.

I asked what I could do for him and he asked me if I could get anymore of the stuff that I had gotten for Janice the day before. I told him that he didn't look like somebody who used junk and asked him why he wanted it. He laughed and told me that he in fact had never used the stuff and that he was just doing a favor for a friend. A friend that didn't want anyone knowing he had anything to do with the stuff. A friend I found out later who was a well known musician and someone I knew quite well.

I told him I'd see what I could do. He handed me five $20 bills saying "I have to run a couple of errands, I'll check back with you later". We both left the flat at the same time and it wasn't more than 20 minutes before I was back.

When after several hours Roger still hadn't shown back up, I decided to head down to the Carousel Ballroom. I put the 10 balloons I'd purchase for him in a small sandalwood stash box on the kitchen table and told Joanne where he could find them on my way out the door.

Finding the stash box sitting in the middle of my bed when I returned later that evening, I opened it to find two $20 bills, five of the balloons and a note saying "These are for you. Thanks for everything, I'll see you soon".

"Wow, that's pretty fucking cool of him" I thought, pocketing the two $20 bills. I then placed the stash box under my bed and promptly forgot about it until about two weeks later when he paid me a return visit.

All of my inquiries as to just exactly who Roger was - if in fact that was his real name - turned up very little information that could be substantiated.

The rumor mill however was working overtime as usual. One of the stories had him being an eccentric millionaire who had made his fortune smuggling hashish in the early part of the 60s. It was said that he still maintained a stash of several thousand pounds of the stuff and that it was buried somewhere in the wilds of Northern California.

Another story portrayed him as an eccentric millionaire genius who was one of the first people to independently synthesize LSD in the United States.

Other stories had him being a combination of the two with the added element that he was a major behind-the-scenes financial backer of one or two of the top San Francisco rock 'n roll bands.

Whatever the case was it soon became abundantly clear that he had no intention of telling me any detailed information about himself whatsoever.

I started to suspect that at least some part of the stories were true on his next visit. The same scenario as before played itself out with him handing me 5 $20s and telling me he'd be back later.

When after a couple of hours he hadn't returned, I once again left the balloons on the kitchen table - this time in a plastic baggie - and went out about my business. This time, however, upon my return I found a large brick of gold stamped hashish wrapped in clear yellow cellophane, two $20 bills, five more of the balloons I had just copped for him and a note saying "Thanks, Enjoy".

I'd never seen so much hashish in my life! It was such a nice gesture. I didn't have the heart to tell him that I never really liked smoking the stuff.

By the time of his sixth visit the old sandalwood stash box under my bed had long since been replaced by a shoebox. A shoe box that now contained two large bricks of hashish - one from Afghanistan and one from Nepal, 30 balloons of heroin, a pound of weed and a wide variety of different colored tabs of acid. All of which I had no interest in whatsoever.

Somewhere about this time it finally dawned on me that I should just start selling him back the balloons that he had left for me instead of going out and getting more of them. Okay, so I'm a little bit slow on the uptake sometimes.

Another person who began to show up at Joanne's fl at on an almost daily basis was my friend Dickie Peterson, the bass player and lead singer of the band Blue Cheer.

Dickie Peterson
Photo Credit - S.F. Archives

Blue Cheer was a power trio that played what at the time could only be described as blues-based psychedelic rock. Nowadays it would be considered heavy metal.

They in fact are considered by many to be the progenitors of punk, heavy metal, and grunge. Jim Morrison of the Doors called the group" the single most powerful band I've ever seen."

The band was thought to have taken its name from a particularly potent brand of LSD made by Owsley called Blue Cheer. In truth they both had very strong connections with Owsley and both appeared on the scene at the same time. Both were named by Owsley who worked very closely with the band and was listed as the producer on their first album.

Dickie and I had been good friends for quite a while. Unfortunately, the nature of our relationship began to change on account of his growing interest and use of substances in the opiate family.

Because of the regular amount of dope that I was now purchasing on behalf of other people, Delicious wanted to start fronting me 20 or 30 bags at a time so I didn't have to come looking for him every time someone wanted something.

Not wanting to get more involved in the whole scene than I already was, I declined the offer. In my mind I was just doing favors for a few people. Little did I realize the devastating effect the drug would have on some of my very closest friends, the community as a whole and eventually myself.

But I'm getting ahead of the story…

Chapter 19

My other favorite place to hang out when I wasn't at the Family Dog was the Fillmore West. This presented a problem for me, however, because unlike the Family Dog I was expected to pay a nominal fee in order to gain access to the premises just like everyone else. I didn't mind the idea of paying the fee per se - because it was well worth the price - it's just that I never seemed to have any money to pay it with. This led me to try and find other means to gain access.

After a thorough investigation I found that I was left only two options.

Option 1: I could go to Bill Graham and ask him for a job which would allow me unlimited access.

Option 2: I could simply sneak in.

Being a fairly clueless 16-year-old with no job history whatsoever and the work ethics of a broken toaster, I decided that option two was my best course of action.

This as it turned out was a lot easier than I expected it to be though for reasons other than my self-supposed cleverness as I was to find out years later from Bill Graham himself.

The fact that I had never once in four years been caught and thrown out should've given me a clue that something else was going on. But I honestly had no idea until I had a chance meeting with Bill 22 years later at the Oakland Coliseum.

The occasion was a Day on the Green concert, featuring Queensryche and Metallica, that drummer Matt Sorum and I had driven up from LA to attend.

The place was the sound platform where Matt and I were hanging out watching the proceedings. Just before Metallica went on stage, Bill Graham glanced at me as he was passing by where we were sitting. To my total surprise Bill turned around and came up to me and said in his usual gruff manner "you know all those times you snuck into my club?" "Yes Bill" I said, feeling like a little kid who'd just been caught with his hand in the cookie jar, "well, I just wanted you to know that I told my guys to let you sneak in. You were too damn young to be on the streets by yourself. I was worried about you." I was completely blown away. I had no idea. I didn't even think he knew who I was. "Thanks Bill" I said barely managing to conceal how choked up I was feeling. Bill was an amazing human being.

Anyway, my first methods of getting into the club involved either trying to sneak past Smitty at the back door or going in with bands that I knew from working at the Newport Festival or The Family Dog. These bands included It's a Beautiful Day, Country Weather, Devils Kitchen, Country Joe and the Fish, 10 Years After, Joe Cocker and the Grease Band, Spirit, Manfred Mann, Tower of Power, Santana, Big Brother and the Grateful Dead. Other times I would attach myself to one or more of the light shows that worked the Family Dog as well as Bill's Club.

Sometimes I would simply walk in the back door and head up the stairs like I owned the place and hope no one stopped me.

When all else failed I would go to Smitty who guarded the back door and tell him that I was there to meet up with friends of mine who were in one of the bands. He would usually give me a suspicious look and make me wait for a few minutes. Eventually he'd let me in.

One night my scheme nearly backfired on me when one of the bands that I told him I was there to meet drove up in the middle of my story. The band was The Who. The minute I saw them I knew I was up shit creek without a paddle because I'd never met any of them in my life.

They arrived in a rented station wagon driven by one of the road crew. The first one out of the car was Roger Daltrey followed by Keith Moon, John Entwistle and a beautiful young English girl and finally Peter Townsend - who emerged from the rear facing 3rd row seat with a martini in his hand.

As for me, I was trapped like a rat. I was so surprised by their unexpected early arrival I was just sort of frozen in my tracks. I quietly watched as the guys unloaded the car and grabbed their bags and proceeded up the long stairway that led to the backstage area.

I was still trying to figure out how I was going to get out of this one when Smitty asked John Entwistle - the last member of the band into the building - if he knew me, telling him that I said I was there to meet up with them. To my great surprise John looked me up and down, looked over at Smitty and said "sure, he's a good lad." He then grabbed my ear like a schoolteacher and said "come on now, up with you'" and proceeded to drag me upstairs by the ear with a mischievous smile on his face.

Still holding me - not too gently - by the ear he led me to the backstage area and asked me my name. I introduced myself and he patted me on the cheek and said "have fun" and went off to get ready for the show.

To say I was stunned by the whole affair would be the epitome of an understatement. I was floored. It felt like some sort of a weird dream. One minute I'm downstairs where it looks like I'm about to be busted for lying and the next minute I'm backstage hanging out with The Who. Curiouser and curiouser…

At first all I could manage to do was to sit down and nervously smile at everyone, but I eventually mustered up enough courage to start talking to the young English girl who had gotten out of the car with the rest of the guys.

It seems that she had been asked at the last minute to come out and do wardrobe for the band when their regular wardrobe lady was suddenly taken ill or pregnant or something similar to that.

She was 18 and about as beautiful as any girl I'd ever seen. Being the suave self-confi dent 16-year-old know-it-all man of the world that every teenage boy imagines himself to be, I could tell instantly that I didn't stand a snowball's chance in hell with this girl. She was incredibly gorgeous, very articulate and spoke with a very sexy English accent. Jackie was her name and she was not quite 2 years older than I was. Luckily for me it turned out that I was totally wrong - about the snowball I mean. To say that we hit it off with each other just doesn't serve the situation well. It was one of those intense young romantic storybook type situations that always seem to end too soon. More than likely though it was simply a case of teenage hormones run rampant. Whatever it was, it was amazing. (fade to black)

We didn't drag ourselves out of bed until about an hour before sound check the next day which is when she had to be back on the job.

The sound check was particularly interesting for me because it gave me a chance to catch up with a couple of my dad's friends that were playing with Woody Herman who was on the bill with The Who along with a local San Francisco band called A.B Skhy. The best part was that I got to hang out with an amazingly mischievous elf named Keith Moon.

Trying to come up with a comparative analogy between Keith and another person with similar qualities would be an exercise in futility. There's never been anyone else like him. He was one of the most animated, hyperactive, charming, witty, insanely lovable madmen that I've ever had the privilege to meet.

My formal introduction to him came when he launched himself from the middle of the stage towards where Jackie and I had been standing watching the band and landed flat on his ass on the edge of the stage with his right hand extended toward me and said "hi, my name's Keith." He then proceeded to vigorously shake hands with me.

I was totally taken aback and completely charmed at the same time. Everyone who ever met him - except for hotel managers - felt the same way about him.

I firmly believe that he was the funniest person on the planet back in those days. Unfortunately, my memories of the short time that I spent with him are vague and fragmented at best. If you're in the least bit familiar with Keith's personality at all you'll understand why. What I do remember is that we talked and drank and laughed so much our sides hurt. By the end of the evening he had given me his phone number, address and an invitation to come stay with him if I ever got to England. He was lovely person.

The next day Jackie and I had breakfast and ran around town till about four o'clock when it was time for sound check again.

Things were a bit frantic for her because the band had to leave early that evening to catch a flight to New York so Pete could appear in court the next day.

It seems Pete had been arrested and charged with assault after knocking a plainclothes policeman off the stage at New York's Fillmore East earlier in the tour, not realizing that the man was a police officer who was trying to explain that the show had to be stopped owing to a fire in the building next door.

That night The Who went on early and played one long set, as opposed to the two back to back 45 minute sets that the bands usually played at the Fillmore.

I stood at the edge of the stage for almost the entire set paying particular attention to John Entwistle's finger work on the bass. At the end of the set I returned to the backstage area were Jackie and I bade each other a tearful goodbye with promises to stay in touch and see each other again soon.

I walked her downstairs to the car and kissed her one last time and watched the car slowly drive away taking her out of my life forever. Even after all these years, I still haven't forgotten her and that in itself is a gift.

Chapter 20

Article from the Oakland Tribune July 3rd 1969

Commune Takes 2nd Life NOVATO

A second child has died as a result of a swimming pool accident at Rancho Olompali. 2 year old Audrey Keller died at Marin County General Hospital yesterday just two days after the death of her 2 year old companion Nika Carter. Both fell into the pool while playing with a tricycle near the edge of the pool. Acting on reports of un-sanitary and unsafe conditions at the Commune, the Marin County Board of Supervisors Tuesday instructed its attorney to begin efforts to evict the residents. The board also asked the county probation officer t o investigate. Novato builder Tim O'Donoghue told the board he would fence off the swimming pool at once and will proceed immediately with plans to develop the area. He said he already has moved residents out of a dormitory branded a fire hazard by county...

In the early evening hours of July 1st I received the devastating news that two of the children at the ranch had been involved in a terrible accident. It was doubly devastating for me because I had brought one of the parents and her child up to the ranch to live and the parents of the other little girl were very close friends of mine.

Near the beginning of 1969 James and I had moved our friend Puanani along with her baby daughter Nika and all of their belongings out of the house on 83 Noe Street and up to Rancho Olompali. A month or so earlier James and Nancy Gurley and I had taken her and her daughter up to the ranch for a visit. She fell in love with the place. It seemed perfect for them. It had its own school and plenty of young children for Nika to play with. Plus it was out of the city.

Because I had introduced her to the ranch I felt horribly guilty about what happened. Sadly it was more of an ominous prelude of things to come than anything else.

Marin County officials had been looking for a way to get everyone off the land for quite awhile and this was a perfect opportunity for them to do it.

Within a couple months all the original people were gone from the ranch - though it continued to be illegally inhabited for quite some time afterwards.

The beautiful dream of Rancho Olompali had come to an end just as the hopes and dreams of the 60s were beginning to crash down around our heads. Within a year almost to the day one of my closest friends would be dead and another would be arrested for second degree murder and I would be deep off into the world of hard drugs...

Chapter 21

On my return to the Fell Street house after having been gone for a few days I found a curious small white envelope sitting on the kitchen table with the words "for Terry, from Jack Frost" written on the front of it. Opening it I found a large single white crystal of what turned out to be Peruvian flake cocaine weighing about a full half ounce. I had heard about this stuff but had actually never seen any. What's more I had no idea where this came from or why someone would leave it for me.

What I did know was that some of the band guys were using it before they went on stage and a folk singer named Dave Van Ronk had done a song about it.

Not knowing what to do with it I waited for Joanne to come home and showed it to her to see if she knew where it came from and how you were supposed to do the stuff. She told me that Roger had come by while I was gone and she thought that he had probably left it for me. As for doing it she thought we should go over to see James.

When I showed the stuff to him his eyes lit up like a kids on Christmas day. He said it was the biggest single crystal that he'd ever seen and that Peruvian fl ake was the best cocaine in the world. He brought out a mirror and a razor blade and took a small amount of it and chopped it up on the mirror. He then divided the chopped up pile into a few small lines and rolled up dollar bill to the shape of a straw and snorted a couple lines. He handed me the mirror and the dollar bill and I too snorted a couple of the lines and passed the mirror to Joanne.

The first thing I noticed was that my nose and front teeth began to get slightly numb. This was closely followed by a mildly euphoric sense of exhilaration.

Not knowing what to expect I kept waiting for something else to happen. When nothing did, I started wondering why so many people were doing it and what all the fuss was about.

Next thing I noticed was that while I didn't particularly think much of the stuff, I nevertheless had an overwhelming desire to do more. Sensing that there was more to this shit than meets the eye I gave the rest of it to James who was over the moon about the stuff. I went back across the Panhandle to the house Joanne I were sharing with the feeling that I had avoided a potentially bad situation. For the time being anyway.

In August another visiting musician who came to stay at our house was Steve Peregrine Took of the band Tyrannosaurus Rex. Steve and I had a blast together, though to tell you the truth I don't remember a lot of what happened exactly. Mostly just vague snippets of events.

What little I do remember seemed to be centered around an ongoing feud taking place between him and his band mate Marc Bolan.

After having met Marc it wasn't hard to see why they were feuding. Marc presented himself as being a very insecure, standoffish, self obsessed snob. Needless to say he didn't endear himself to very many of the people he met in San Francisco.

One incident in particular stands out clearly in my mind. It took place in the large upstairs backstage area of the Family Dog that was used as a shared dressing room by all the bands.

Steve-Peregrin-Took
Photo Credit - Berkeley Barb Archive

The room was filled with quite a few people including Alan Watts who was standing quite near the entrance. In the middle of the room was of very large meeting table that could easily seat up to 20 people and Steve and I were standing at the far end of the table when Marc entered the room and started to cause a scene with Steve. Without the slightest sign of perturbation Steve very casually bent down and picked up a full can of beer from an ice filled container next to us and nailed Marc right between the eyes with it from across the room. It was fucking amazing! Alan Watts, who had been standing right next to Marc, almost fell on the floor he was laughing so hard. It was brilliant! The timing was perfect! Steve's aim was impeccable and Marc so deserved it! Needless to say it was one of last times they played together.

It was some time right after this event that things took another very dramatic turn towards the weird.

Chapter 22

Shortly after Steve and Marc left town, I found myself back over at Paula's helping make up a new batch of blotter acid, when another bizarre incident occurred.

During the five or so hours I had been preparing the new batch I placed several drops of pure liquid LSD on my tongue. At some point later that evening after everyone had gone out I began to hear a very low frequency rumbling sound that seemed to be coming from several hundred feet directly above the house. As I listened it began to descend getting closer and closer until it seemed to be mere feet above the house. Suddenly the house became flooded with an extremely bright white light coming through all of the Windows and door cracks from outside of the building. It reminded me very much of a scene that I saw years later in a movie called Close Encounters of The Third Kind. In this case the appliances in the house were unaffected.

As I stood in the hallway stunned by the intense display of light and sound, the front door began to slowly open of its own accord, revealing an intensely lit, though completely empty front landing through which several seconds later, entered a short, round, curly headed little lady named Mama Bear.

She walked directly up to me and said "I can't stay around any longer, the Mother has become very ill, and it's time for me to go". 'The Mother' I thought? What does she mean by 'The Mother'?

She then handed me a silver and turquoise necklace in the shape of a six pointed star. She kissed me on the cheek and said "I love you" then turned on her heels and walked straight out the door leaving it wide open.

The instant she got out of sight the bright lights that had been flooding through the windows winked out and the sound began to take off back up into the sky.

Gathering my wits about me I ran outside as fast as I could to see what was going on only to find a completely empty street and a clear star filled sky that contained nothing out of the ordinary.

I did a quick scan of the area as I ran to the corner to see if I could catch up with Mama Bear. She was nowhere in sight. I then ran down the street in the opposite direction but was still unable to locate her or any other living creature for that matter.

The distance between where I was standing and where she disappeared couldn't have been more than 25 feet. It hadn't been more than 2 or 3 seconds after she was out of my sight that I ran out and looked for her. It seemed totally impossible, yet she had somehow managed to vanish without a trace.

I just stood there in the middle of the street holding the silver and turquoise necklace trying to figure out what the hell had just happened. I had the weirdest feeling that I had somehow stumbled into an episode of the twilight zone...

Now, having Mama Bear show up in the middle of what could have been easily construed as a UFO incident was tantamount to finding out that your 93 year old wheelchair-bound grandmother had just been picked to represent Norway as a ski-jumper in the winter olympics. In other words, it was the last thing in the world that you would've expected to happen. It was completely out of context and totally absurd.

And therein lays a perfect example of the sort of zany quality that is an integral aspect of all of these bizarre events. It's what is referred to by Terence McKenna and others, as "The Cosmic Giggle." It is always a part of these peak psychedelic experiences. It's also what makes it so hard to talk to anyone else about these things simply because no one would take you seriously if you did. Or so I thought.

As it turns out there were thousands of other people having the same type of experiences. However most of them were unwilling to talk about what was happening for this exact same reason.

The most disconcerting aspect of the whole incident was that it was as censorious and tactile as any other everyday experience of what we call normal reality. There was no fuzzy far-off visionary dreamlike quality to it like that which usually accompanies the use of narcotics. No fog brained awareness like that of marijuana. It was sharp, crystal clear, immediate in its intensity and really quite amusing. It was also nowhere near as astoundingly bizarre as things would reveal themselves to be in the very near future.

Chapter 23

On August 19th we had another Commons meeting at The Family Dog. While the meetings always involved a very diverse group of people, this one was over the top! Sometimes the meetings themselves were far more spectacular than any of the events that were planned. At this meeting in particular, a short list of the participants included:

Ken Kesey and Ken Babbs and the Merry Pranksters, Alan Watts, Timothy Leary, Allen Ginsberg, the Grateful Dead, the New Riders of the Purple Sage, Big Brother, the Jefferson Airplane, Stephen Gaskin, Master Choy, Quicksilver, Devils Kitchen, Osceola, the Charlatans, Country Joe, it's a Beautiful Day, Santana, Elvin Bishop, Mike Bloomfi eld, A.B. Skhy, the Congress of Wonders, Barry Melton, the Ace of cups, the Young Bloods, Commander Cody, the Sons of Champlin, Tom and Rachel Donahue, Chet Helms, Magic Sam, Jerry Abrams, representatives of all the major light shows and the wives, children, friends and dogs of all the participants.

The scene was hilariously chaotic with children and barking dogs running pell-mell through the crowd led by a skipping Allen Gins-berg. The late arrival of the Prankster's bus turned the already chaotic situation into one of pure bedlam with the two Kens - Kesey and Babbs - leading an anarchistic charge against any semblance of impending order.

It's totally astounding that anything got done at all. But somehow in the middle of all the confusion we (the Commons) managed to hammer out a schedule for the venue covering the next couple months.

As the day progressed towards evening, this amazing, good-natured free-for-all ended up turning into a long protracted jam session with members of the Grateful Dead, Jefferson Airplane, A.B. Skhy and Elvin Bishop that lasted well into the night.

Two days later on August 21 I achieved the ripe old age of 17. I celebrated this momentous occasion by nearly missing it completely. If it hadn't have been for Nancy Gurley and Linda Gravenites (wife of Chicago Blues man Nick Gravenites) both of whom appeared on the doorstep of the Fell Street house bearing birthday gifts of fresh home-baked bread wrapped in hand dyed purple lace, a life-sized replica of a human skull and a hand carved Tibetan bone ring, it would've slipped what was left of my mind, completely.

Ever since I'd met Nancy Gurley she did her best to look after me by always trying to make sure I had food and a place to stay. She was my Guardian Angel and became a sort of second mother to me. I loved her dearly.

Nancy was an amazing lady and one of the most progressive women of her time. She was the archetype of the highly intellectual, fully liberated earth mother and she was the role model for so many women back then. Especially Janis.

She defied all stereo types and broke all the molds. Her style of dress, the jewelry she wore, the way she carried herself and every- thing she did was emulated by the counter culture women of San Francisco. And for good reason too. She and James had been part of the scene since the days before it even existed:

Before moving from Detroit to San Francisco, James had entered the Catholic Brothers of the Holy Cross seminary school, where he studied for four years, with the goal of becoming a priest. In the meantime, he was playing folk gigs at many of the Detroit coffee houses like the Cup of Socrates. In 1957 he met and fell in love with a Wayne State University, straight A student named Nancy, who worked there as a waitress. Soon after he gave up on the ministry. Shortly after their marriage they began traveling around the country and down into Mexico. They eventually ended up in Big Sur on the California coast.

In 1962 He and Nancy settled in the North Beach District of San Francisco. Here they came into contact with the coffee-house circuit that was part of the "beat" scene. James soon found himself playing folk and traditional country blues. It was during this early coffee-house period in 1963 that James met a young Texas folk and blues singer named Janis Joplin with whom he would later have a personal and working relationship.

Nancy-Gurley-Hongo-Gurley
Photo Credit - Sam Andrew

There is enough information out there about this stuff already, so I don't really think I need to get into it any further...

I didn't have much to do the next day because the three-day outdoor Wild West Festival that I was supposed to help out at in Golden Gate Park was canceled at the last minute. So having nothing better to do I decided to see if I could actually get away with walking into the dark seedy looking 40s era bar on Haight Street called the Pall Mall and ordering a drink.

Armed with my friend Dickie Peterson's ID - which he had left with me in lieu of payment for certain items - I walked in and sat down expecting to be tossed out any minute.

I didn't realized how unprepared I was for the experience until the bartender walked over to me and asked me what I wanted. I didn't have a clue what to say to him. I'd never been in a bar before. I didn't know the name of any mixed alcoholic drinks. I must've looked like a deer caught in the headlights because the bartender began eyeing me suspiciously.

I glanced at the front door with the idea of making a fast exit, when in a moment of inspired brilliance I suddenly blurted out that famous old cowboy movie bar scene line "give me a shot of Rye whiskey".

The bartender raised one eyebrow and looked over his shoulder at an old bottle of Rock and Rye sitting on the shelf behind him. Shaking his head he turned back towards me with a smile that reached only the right side of his face and put a napkin down on the bar and walked away.

I pulled a five dollar bill out of my pocket and placed it on the bar just as the bartender - still wearing that crooked half smile - returned with my drink.

There was something about that smile that made me feel very uncomfortable so I decided to finish the drink as quickly as possible and be on my way.

Grabbing the shot glass I decided that I would down it all at once like they do in the movies. This however turned out to be a huge mistake. The stuff was horrible! It tasted like a mixture of rubbing alcohol and pancake syrup with just a hint of battery acid.

In an attempt to keep from choking and coughing out loud I turned my now watery eyed, beet red face towards the door and headed out onto the street as quickly as possible - leaving my momentary interest in hard alcohol and the five dollar bill behind in the bar.

It would be almost 2 years before I set foot in the Pall Mall again.

The following Sunday Joanne held one of her regular HP Lovecraft reading parties. The format was that we would all gather in the main room in front of the altar - where the skull that Nancy had given me now resided as the centerpiece - and sit cross-legged in a circle with each of us taking turns reading the book aloud. Those present that day were, our dear friend Val Fuentes from the band It's A Beautiful Day, Dickie Peterson from Blue Cheer, another close friend of ours named Idaho, our roommate Bruce and most of the members of the band Devils Kitchen.

On this particular day the story we had chosen was called "The Haunter of The dark". It took place in Providence, Rhode Island and revolved around the Church of Starry Wisdom were the cult in the story used an ancient artifact known as the Shining Trapezo-hedron to summon a terrible being from the depths of time and space.

It was a very cool and very creepy story, made even more creepy for us by the fact that at the exact instant that we were reading about Blake - the main character - being attacked by the evil dark Nyarlathotep a small earthquake hit the area knocking some precariously perched books from the shelves down on us - sending us all running into the streets terror-stricken.

In hindsight it was absolutely hilarious. At the time though it was one of the scariest things I've ever experienced! Well that, and public school... On second thought, public school was much worse!

Not long afterwards I spent a couple days with Chick Churchill the keyboard player in the band 10 Years After - who were doing three nights at the Fillmore West.

I first met Chick a year earlier at the Fillmore when I lent him a hand during their load in - helping to carry and set up his Hammond B3 organ.

I had originally gone to the gig with my friend Greg Douglas' band Country Weather - who were on the bill with them. I'll never forget the impression that was left on my imaginative 16-year-old mind when Alvin Lee - the guitar player of the band - arrived at the gig that night wearing a full-length fur coat and satin pants with a beautiful blonde girl on each arm, each of whom was carrying one of his guitars.

"Holy Shit!" I thought, "Where the hell do you sign up for that gig?" If I'd had any doubts earlier about what I wanted to do with the rest of my life that dispelled every one of them. A bit juvenile I must admit, but I was a teenager after all and I really didn't have any other goals at the time.

Chapter 24

October '69...

Everything written in this narrative so far has been leading up to this pivotal point I am about to relate to you. Everything that occurred after this point was either the direct result of or has been colored in some way by that event.

The event led me through the depths of very dark drug addiction and into the light of nearly 28+ years of sobriety. It also led me through years of research into such diverse fields as: comparative religion, Eastern spirituality and philosophy, world mythology, shamanism, the latest findings of quantum and astrophysics, ethno botany and finally the field of neuroscience. In particular the study of the 5-hydroxytryptamine receptor sites in the brain. But more about all this later...

This pivotal point began at the house on Fell Street and ended at the Family Dog on The Great Highway. The occasion was a three day gig that took place on October 7th, 8th & 9th 1969 called "The Holy Man Jam" that featured: Steve Gaskin, Timothy Leary, Asoke Fakir, Malachi, Alan Watts, Swami Satchidananda, Pir Vilayat

Inayat Khan, Lazarus, Michael Lorimer, It's A Beautiful Day, Phoenix, Sufi Sam, Master Choy, Rabbi Schlomo Carl Bach, Hare Krishnas from the San Francisco temple, several visiting Tibetan monks, Reverend Henslee, a group of Catholic Monks, Allen Noonan, Jim Kimmel, Golden Toad, Tup Fisher, Osceola, Chiran Jeed, Garden of Delights, Sweet Misery, Jerry Abrams Headlights, The Holy Sea, Rainbow Gem, Sebastian Moon, Dr Zarkov, May Flower, John Adams and Magana Baptiste, and a whole lot of other folks not listed.

I left for the gig with Joanne and my friends: Val Fuentes - whose band It's A Beautiful Day was playing there that night - and the now band less Steve Peregrine Took recently of Tyrannosaurus Rex who had arrived the day before on his way back to London.

Before leaving Steve and I decided to drop some of the blotter acid I had just made up. As usual, I took a slightly heftier dose than most sane people would normally consider taking.

The blotters we'd been making up had become progressively stronger over the last year. So much so that what was once a single dose per square was now four doses per square, each one having dividing lines being drawn on them to indicate that they should be divided into quarters.

The main problem with blotter acid was the potential inconsistency in dosage from hit to hit. While the size of the drop of liquid that was applied to each of the squares of blotter paper was the same amount, the amount of LSD contained in each drop could vary greatly with the obvious result being that some hits were much stronger than others. By doing the math and taking into account the known problem with consistency, we figured that each full square of blotter paper should theoretically contain somewhere between 800 and 1000 μg of pure LSD.

Truthfully we had no idea what the strength was since we had no way of measuring it except by doing a bio assay i.e. taking it ourselves.

Shortly after Steve and I piled into the back seat of Val's Volkswagen I began to come onto the acid. By the time we got to the beach I was in the Jeweled Lotus realm of Amitabha Buddha or at least a close facsimile thereof.

All the things of normal everyday reality that I saw suddenly became transformed into beautifully colored, perfectly jeweled forms of themselves. This included people as well. In truth, words utterly fail in the attempt to describe how amazingly beautiful everything was.

I had taken a lot of high doses of LSD before and things had become very colorful and beautiful, but nowhere near what was happening here. It felt like I had walked into a hitherto unknown world or parallel dimension that was coexistent with ours, a magical world where there was no strife and no ego, a place where anything and everything was possible. It was crystal clear perfect in all aspects and excruciatingly familiar.

The most astonishing aspect of the place - besides its absolute beauty - was the fact that I seemed to know this place very well. I felt like I'd been there before, yet how could that be?

The normally cold weather that one experiences at the beach in San Francisco now felt as perfect as any mid-summer nights Eve. I stood gazing out at the jeweled sunset and watching the perfect surfers ride perfect waves.

Just as the sun was starting to go down a group of three or four strangers walked up to me and said "watch this, we can all make the sun go up and down on the horizon." Without even a second thought to consider how ludicrous the whole idea was we all looked out at the setting sun and laughingly chanted "uuuuuuup!" and watched in amazement as the sun slowly rose above the western horizon. Having raised it to a sufficient height above the water we decided to try the other direction and chanted "dowwwn!" To which the sun responded -making us laugh all the more. We continued this activity for several more minutes until my group of newly found friends decided to bid me adieu and continued on their way.

Sounds crazy right? Well, as the old saying goes "you ain't seen nothing yet!"

At about the same time that my new friends were departing, that sort of telepathic type voice of the logos that originally began speaking to me at the house in Muir woods, spoke to me and said that it was now time for me to go inside the building.

As I passed through the entrance way I very clearly heard my name announced over the PA system followed by the cheering of a large crowd. As I rounded the corner into the main hall I was confronted by a roomful of exquisitely beautiful, clapping, cheering people who all seemed to be waiting for me to enter the room. As if this wasn't disconcerting enough, interspersed throughout the crowd was a small group of nine foot tall white robed beings, whose beauty was beyond the capabilities of all human imagination.

While their appearance was quite androgynous, I did get the feeling that some were in fact male and others female. They all wore long white robes that covered them from shoulder to ground. Each of them held a long thin upright golden staff with a small trident on the end. On or about their person each of them had several symbols or glyphs that I took to be of some sort of spiritual nature. They were blonde light-skinned and of humanoid appearance with a radiant beauty that was so exquisite that it was almost too painful to look at, yet you couldn't take your eyes off of them.

I was so astonished by their appearance that I was frozen in my tracks. The odd thing was that it wasn't their physical appearance that startled me but where they had appeared that had me completely freaked out.

Imagine coming home one evening to suddenly find that a giant redwood tree has unaccountably sprouted up through the middle of your house. You are familiar with your house and you are familiar with redwood trees equally as well. Finding one growing in the middle of your house is another story entirely. It just doesn't compute.

The oddest thing was that I seemed to be very familiar with who they were - just not with them being in the surroundings they were in at the time.

The first words out of my mouth were "you guys aren't supposed to be here" - which even to me seemed like an odd thing to say. At this point I started to get pretty freaked out. It soon became clear that my surprised emotional state was not helping the situation in the least.

The tall beings then attempted to reassure me that everything was all right and that I had nothing to be afraid of. Unfortunately, by this time I was deeply and uncontrollably in the grips of astonishment and fear. After a few more attempts to calm me down one of them walked over to me, bent down and smiled and very gently said "if you're going to be afraid, you're going to have to leave". I looked up at the being with tears beginning to show in my eyes and said "I know, I can't help it, I'm sorry" and turned around and headed for the front door. The last thing I heard before I hit the street was a very disappointed sounding "ahh…" from the crowd who had welcomed me a short time earlier.

The moment I hit the street everything changed back to its normal everyday dingy looking state of being. The weather had once again become cold and foggy. I was left with the feeling that I had been given an amazing opportunity and that I had completely failed to make use of it. I felt stunned and devastated. I had been shown the brass ring and had failed to grasp it. I felt like Parsival - the Knight in Wolfram von Eschenbach's Grail legend - who had been lead to the Grail Castle and failed the test…

Once again I found myself in that familiar "what the hell am I supposed to do with that?" situation. This time, however, I found it impossible to just shrug it off. The implications were far too staggering to ignore:

Was the planet populated by a whole other group of entities that most humans were previously unaware of?

Through the use of psychedelics had I somehow been able to tune the dial of awareness enough to be able to see them?

Or had my brain - under the influence of psychedelics manufactured a virtual reality world that I was capable of walking into and inhabiting for a short period of time?

If so was our everyday experience of reality exactly the same thing only under the influence of serotonin instead of LSD. If any of this was true it meant that everything that we think we know about the nature of reality is utterly and completely wrong.

The most obvious answer was that I was quite simply out of my fucking mind.

The problem was that I didn't feel like I was out of my mind. Confused, astonished, yes! But out of my mind? No. Something else was going on here. I'd known that since I was a little kid. Now it seemed that I had accidentally stumbled onto something that could very well prove my suspicions. At the very least it was certainly worthy of further investigation.

While the scenario may sound like a madman's dream, the experience somehow made more sense and felt more real than anything else I have experienced in my life.

This, however, put me in a very, very tough position. While I felt it to be a quite valid and real experience I also very clearly understood that it was not something that I could discuss with just anyone at that time. Not if I didn't want to find myself being handed a one-way ticket to the California state mental hospital at Camarillo.

It wasn't until many years later that I finally understood the full implications of a statement Alan Watts made one night at the Avalon ballroom when he said:

"The understanding of mystical experience is one of the most dangerous experiences in the world for the person who cannot contain it. It's like putting 1,000,000 Volts through your razor, you blow your mind and it stays blown..."

Well, that's me all over. I'd seen something that I couldn't explain and found impossible to ignore. I felt like I had stumbled onto a secret that nobody was supposed to know anything about and that I couldn't tell anyone about. All of my basic assumptions about the true nature of reality had been called into question, closely examined, found horribly lacking and unceremoniously thrown out the window - leaving me no place to stand. All I had left were thousands of unanswerable questions racing through my head and no way to turn them off.

This is not an enviable situation for anyone not prepared for it to find themselves in, let alone a self-professed 17-year-old pseudo-genius with delusions of rock stardom. I don't know if anyone else knows this, but it's pretty hard to be in a rock band if you're confi ned to a padded cell - unless, of course, you ended up there after the fact.

A couple days later I was still feeling like a shellshock victim so I decided to take a walk to clear my head. As I was walking down Delmar Street towards the Haight I noticed a tall thin barefoot woman standing in an open doorway wearing a 40s style slip dress and smoking a cigarette. As I got closer I recognized that it was Della, the ex-girlfriend of my old friend Bones.

I had met Della the first week I arrived in San Francisco and had only run into her once or twice since then. As I got closer she smiled at me and without a word turned away, motioning me to follow her inside. I was a bit taken aback by this invitation. While our previous interactions had always been cordial, she always seemed a bit aloof and standoffish towards me.

As I entered the flat she pointed me towards a large overstuffed couch and headed for the kitchen, asking me if I would like some tea. I nodded my ascent and turned my attention to the television set where I soon found myself totally engrossed in an episode of Hogan's Heroes.

When she hadn't returned by the time the episode was over, I wandered into the kitchen. There I found her bent over the kitchen table with her back to me. As I got closer she straightened up and handed me a rolled up dollar bill and said "Do you want some"?

I looked at the tabletop and noticed a line of brown-ish powder on the surface of a small mirror. I accepted the dollar bill and bent down and began snorting a line. "What is it" I asked? "Heroin" she said as I finished the line.

I found it a bit ironic that I had been going out and copping quite a bit of this stuff for people over the last year and yet I had never even seen what was inside of the balloons it came in.

20 minutes later I was in her bathroom throwing up. 10 minutes after that all thoughts of hyper-dimensional beings and speculations about the true nature of reality had magically vanished from my mind along with every other care or concern that I had.

Just as LSD had the capability of opening you up to higher levels of awareness, heroin had its own peculiar way of bludgeoning whatever level of awareness you had down into a small fuzzy pinpoint of unawareness. A fuzzy unawareness that was easy to maintain as long as you didn't run out of the stuff.

Right then and there I decided on a new course of action. Instead of searching for the answer to just what the hell was going on here, I decided that I would now simply run away from whatever it was and do the best I could to ignore it! It seemed like a straightforward elegantly simple plan. What could possibly go wrong?

When I was finally able to gather my wits about me, I thanked Della and headed down the road towards the basement flat on Fell Street. When I finally got to my room I laid down on the floor and stared up at the ceiling tapestry.

I quickly nodded off but was soon awakened by the presence of someone standing over me. When I opened my eyes I found myself staring into the face of the most beautifully seductive wild haired woman that I've ever seen. As I held her in my gaze she smiled to reveal a mouthful of beautifully perfect fang like teeth. I instantly realized who she was and what I was looking at.

Since the beginning of time, native shaman from all parts of the world have been telling us that everything has a spirit. The rocks, the trees, the rivers, the birds, the fish - everything. It all has its own spirit and what I was looking into the face of was the spirit of the opium poppy.

She was impossibly beautiful. Irresistibly alluring and absolutely deadly to anyone who didn't exercise extreme care when entering her playground.

I closed my eyes for a moment and when I opened them again she was gone, just as I expected. Hallucination? Absolutely! Though a very telling one. From a Jungian point of view she would've been the archetypal spirit representing Heroin. From my point of view she represented trouble. Unfortunately, trouble was something I hadn't had much luck staying away from so far and there just happened to be quite a bit of it sitting in a shoe box 3 feet from my head.

Chapter 25

It's surprising even to me how quickly I found myself off into the deep end of things. Within a week, I accepted D's offer to start fronting me dope. By the end of the month I had quite a considerable amount of money and almost all of my friend Dickie Peterson's musical equipment.

Dickie, who had acquired a substantial habit over the last couple years, had recently fallen on hard times and had begun trading me musical equipment - and anything else he had of value - for dope. This included his wallet and ID.

The ID was probably the most useful thing I got from him at the time because I didn't have one. It also goes a long way towards explaining why the cops thought my name was Richard Allan Peterson when I got arrested a few months later.

Up until that time I had been snorting the stuff, but it didn't take long for me to realize that I was already pretty strung out. It wasn't long afterwards that I had to start shooting stuff to keep up with my rapidly growing habit.

The first time I ever shot up was also the first time that I ever heard the Rolling Stones album "Gimme' Shelter." I had gone over to

James's house to bring him a couple of bags. When I got there I found him in possession of a box full of new syringes and the Rolling Stones new album.

I watched James fix up a bag of dope and shoot it. I then ask him if he thought it was better to shoot the stuff or snort it. He said that if you shot it, you didn't have to do quite as much as you did when you snorted it. "Besides" He said "the rush is much better if you shoot it". Having some dope of my own with me I asked him to show me how to do it. He showed me how much water to use, how to cook it up and how to draw it up through a piece of cotton. He then helped me find a vein.

Just as I was starting to come on to the stuff, he put on the Rolling Stones album. It seemed like the perfect soundtrack for the trip that I was taking. A trip I soon found out that was leading me nowhere fast.

With every new drug, there comes a new crowd of people and a new group of running partners. One of my new running partners was a very nice, very talented young guy named Ricky Stevens who was the lead singer of the band Tower of Power.

I'd met Rick a few months earlier at one of their gigs at the Fillmore and it wasn't long before we became the proverbial partners in crime. We always seemed to be out on the streets together involved in some sort of a hustle.

If we weren't hustling dope, we were out hustling chicks. If we weren't hustling chicks, we are out trying to find the next big surefire hustle or hanging out at one of the clubs.

During my association with Ricky I came into contact with a lot of well-known musicians who always seemed to be looking for a place to cop dope. One night when Ricky and I ventured backstage at the Fillmore during a Johnny Winters show, I ended up selling all 20 bags that I had with me to the people that were hanging out there.

Two years before it had been marijuana and LSD. Now it was heroin and cocaine. Unfortunately, because the government had lied to us so much about how bad LSD and marijuana were, I don't think any of us actually believed that heroin was as bad as they said it was. Boy were we wrong.

December 31, 1969 found me at the Fillmore hanging out with my friend Val Fuentes at a gig where It's a Beautiful Day were playing with Santana, Elvin Bishop and Joy of Cooking. It was a really fun show though Carlos, Val, Chapito and myself managed to piss off the lead singer of Joy of Cooking pretty badly during their set.

The stage set up at the Fillmore was a fairly typical theatre style, having a large backdrop curtain that screened the backstage area from the front of the house and a separate dressing room area that could be entered from the right-hand side of the stage.

On this particular night all of Santana's Latin percussion instruments were set up directly behind the curtain. At the end of Joy of Cooking's set they did a song that I believe was called "Did you go downtown" that featured drummer Fritz Kasten and percussionist Ron Wilson. I was standing in the backstage area right next to where all the percussion instruments were set up, lightly tapping on one of the conga drums keeping time with the music, when Carlos walked up, winked at me and started playing one of the other congas himself. Within a few short seconds we were joined by Val and Chapito, one of Santana's percussionists. In the blink of an eye we were all exuberantly jamming away with the band members on stage from our hidden position behind the curtain.

At the end of the song as we were starting to walk away when the curtain was suddenly thrown back and we were confronted by a very irate Terry Garthwaite - the lead singer guitar player of the band - who looked for all the world like she was going to tear all of our heads off. I was preparing myself for the worst when she suddenly pushed past us and stormed off towards the dressing rooms. Feeling a little bit guilty we all looked at each other with a great sense of relief and we all went about our business. It was pretty funny really, unfortunately not to everyone...

Chapter 26

Have you ever noticed how quickly things can get out of control and how bad they can get before suddenly going to hell completely? Well, all you had to do was take a walk down Haight Street if you wanted to see a perfect example of this in action. The place had gone from a quaint hippie neighborhood to a seedy drug infested slum in the span of less than two years. I, unfortunately, was one of the people that was helping to give the neighborhood it's bad name.

As the winter of 1970 rolled around it become necessary for me to spend extended periods of time on Haight Street in an attempt to stem the growing tide of drug related traffic that was starting to show up at the fell Street house. I started splitting my time up between staying at the Fell Street house and 83 Noe Street where I had regained possession of the front room.

Since I had all the drugs I could possibly want, and two places to live, I had to find something else to spend my ill gotten gains on. After careful examination of all my priorities, it became abundantly clear that the first thing I needed to do was expand my comic book collection.

Most of the stuff I had in my collection were Marvel comics - ones that were on the more obscure side.

When I finally sold my entire collection to Jerry Garcia a couple years later I had complete runs of Dr. Strange, Captain America, the Avengers, Thor, the X-men and Nick Fury Agent of S.H.I.E.L.D. as well as a few short runs like the Silver Surfer, Captain Mar-vell and the SubMariner. I had a few obscure DC comics as well, The Haunted Tank, The Losers and Sargent Rock.

It's funny but every once in a while I still slip into collector mode and find myself deeply involved in the quest to find certain objects.

It's not the actual acquisition of the objects per se that's fun. It's the search itself. The research you do and the following of the trail that leads you to the find that is the exciting part of it. It's sort of like being a treasure hunter I suppose. Though as far as I'm concerned once I complete a collection I lose all interest in it and quickly look to sell it in order to finance my next quest, which for me turned out to be WWII German uniforms. But that's another story...

Along with my newly elevated financial situation came a heightened awareness of the police and their heightened awareness of me. It didn't take me long to learn the names of every narcotics officer assigned to the neighborhood. Most of them played by the rules and did their job honestly. A couple of them though played by their own rules and did whatever they liked. If these guys wanted you off the streets they had no qualms about planting evidence on you in order to get a conviction.

It also didn't take long for me to learn the names of the other guys that were dealing dope on the street. There was 'Chinese Sam' who was actually Japanese - a young mulatto guy called ' Little Tommy' from Detroit - 'Found' a young Canadian guy that hailed from Newfoundland - Redhead Charlie a little white guy from god knows where - a brother from the Fillmore district named Thaddeus - a 25-year-old white chick with 3 young children named 'Trina' and of course myself.

Now before you start thinking that I'm trying to glorify this type of lifestyle let me put you straight. This type of existence is the most bleak, desperate - and for me - mind numbingly depressing situation anyone could ever find themselves in. It ain't fun, hip or cool no matter what some idiot rapper tells you. Trying to dodge the cops and having to be on the constant alert for the scams people would come up with to rip you off is bad enough by itself. If you add that to the fact that at any moment some desperate junkie was liable to rob you at gunpoint then you'll realize that there is nothing fun or cool about it.

Another problem was that a lot of the people from the original neighborhood were dying right and left because of the shit. It's amazing how desperate people can get when they're strung out. There was a constant line of people trying to trade me everything from diamond rings to exotic handguns for dope. Hell, one guy actually traded me a beautifully running 3.8 Jaguar that was in near perfect condition along with the pink slip for 10 bags of dope.

Of course, a month later the car was stolen from me at gunpoint, but what the hell, I didn't have a drivers license anyway.

By the beginning of the summer of 1970 the amount of drug-related robberies in the neighborhood had increased to such an extent that many of us felt that we had no other option but to arm ourselves.

This added a whole new level of paranoia to the scene, most of which was caused by one guy named Fast Joey.

Joey had gone from being an annoying pain in the ass to a source of major concern for most of us. Particularly so after one of his numerous attempted drug robberies went awry and he ended up shooting a couple of people in the Panhandle.

We all felt pretty relieved when he was arrested. But when he showed back up on the streets after a couple weeks we realized we had a serious problem on our hands. It also seemed pretty clear to us that the police weren't really in any hurry to get him off the streets because he was doing a better job of getting rid of dope dealers than they were.

Sadly his reign of intimidation didn't come to an end until he finally murdered one of our original group of dealers a couple years later.

Chapter 27

If you didn't pay too much attention to the calendar you would be hard put to tell what time of year it was in San Francisco judging by the weather alone. For 11 months out of the year the average daytime temperature was always somewhere between 57° and 67°F except for the month of September when it once got as high as 101° though the usual monthly average for September was 70°.

For a few weeks I had been planning to take a trip back up to Olompali to enjoy some real summer weather and see my old friend Terry from Petaluma, who was still caretaking the horses that were left up at the ranch. I also wanted to see if any of the old people had stuck around after Don McCoy's group had been ordered to vacate the place.

I got my opportunity on the Fourth of July when James and Nancy offered to drop me off at the ranch on their way up to the Russian River. James decided that he wanted to stop doing dope and he and Nancy both thought that the Russian River would be a good place to do it.

I arrived at their house at about 10 o'clock in the morning and squeezed into the back seat of their 1965 Toyota Land Cruiser that was packed full of camping gear.

By the time we turned into the driveway at Olompali it was about 11:30 AM. The place looked deserted so we swung open the gate and drove up into the main area.

I was horrified at how bad the place looked. There was garbage strewn all around the buildings and many of the windows were broken. The organic garden had been completely neglected and the once beautifully kept grounds were totally overgrown.

About 5 min. after we arrived we were confronted by a couple of seedy looking hippie types that told us that they were the caretakers and that we were trespassing on private property.

When I told them who we were and that I used to live there, they lightened up a bit and informed me that Terry was not living there but that he did stop by twice a day to make sure the horses were fed and watered. I asked them if I could stick around to see if Terry showed up and they said that it was ok with them.

Nancy gave me a big hug and kiss goodbye, saying that they would be back in about a week as she got into the front seat of the Toyota. I jumped on the back bumper of their Land Cruiser and rode down to the front gate so I could open it for them and close it after they left. As they drove off down the highway I waved goodbye to them and I closed the gate, little realizing that I would never see Nancy again.

I got back to Fell Street the next afternoon to find everyone in hysterics. When I was finally able to get a coherent word out of anyone I was told that Nancy Gurley was dead and James was being held in jail on second-degree murder charges.

I just went numb. It was almost a year ago to the day that we got the news that Baby Audrey and Nika had drowned in the swimming pool at Olompali. Now Nancy was gone as well.

It wasn't until a couple days later that we were able to get the complete story about what happened. It seems that James had taken along $100 worth of heroin. They spent the afternoon drinking and rafting down the Russian River. They then set up their camp site later on that afternoon. Shortly after they were finished setting up James decided it was time to break out the dope he had with him. As the story goes, James was so wasted from drinking that he missed his own vein entirely. Nancy, however, wasn't so lucky. The heroin was quite strong and her tolerance was low. James scored a perfect hit on her. As Nancy started to read a story to their son Hongo she suddenly fell forward. James rushed her to the nearest hospital but by the time he got her there she was already dead.

When the police arrived to investigate the death, James was so distraught that he told them everything that had happened and handed them the rest of heroin he had in his possession. James was then arrested and charged with second degree murder because he had injected her with the dope.

For me the hopeful optimistic dream of the 1960s was well and truly over. It had somehow morphed into a huge fucking nightmare - a fact that was hammered into me very clearly when a couple weeks later I found myself being chased down and tackled by Officer Garrett on the corner of Haight Street and Cole.

And this brings us to where the story began...

Chapter 28

The story of Synanon...

Shortly after being released into the custody of my father by the Clark County court, he packed me up and drove me to the *Club Casa del Mar* - a large beachside hotel in Santa Monica California that now served as the headquarters for what was initially a drug rehabilitation program.

Founded by Charles E."Chuck" Dederich Synanon was originally a community family home for individuals who voluntarily assisted one another through the experience of drug withdrawal and rehabilitation. Many of its members had criminal backgrounds and quite a few of them had served time in prison. Whether they had run afoul of the law or not, they all shared a common trait. They all had failed to stop doing drugs through the use of traditional mental health services.

Synanon had a highly controversial therapeutic counseling style called Attack Therapy that had its believers and critics both in and out of the traditional mental health community.

By the time I got to their door they were already showing signs of becoming the dictatorially run authoritarian cult that would run afoul of the law a short time later.

Upon my arrival I was ushered into an office where I was told that I had to sign an agreement that stated that everything that I owned and any money that I made from then on belonged to Synanon. I was also informed that since I was a heroin addict I had no hope of having a full recovery and I was therefore expected to live there for the rest of my life. They then told my father that he should not try to contact me for at least six months and hurriedly ushered him out of the building.

The thing that I found the most odd was that everyone - women included - had their heads completely shaved. The scary part was that they all talked like brainwashed zombies.

The Zombie aspect of the whole thing became very apparent to me on my first day when I ran into my best childhood friend Steve Merket. Unbeknownst to me, Steve had been in Synanon almost a year already. It was one of the eeriest experiences I've ever had and one that really scared the shit out of me.

Here was my best friend - who had been living in this place for only one year - and they had somehow managed to completely remove all traces of his personality. He was now completely incapable of expressing himself in any terms other than those expressed in the jingoistic cliché ridden recordings of Chuck Dederich that were piped throughout the building 24 hours a day.

I wasn't particularly happy when I first walked into the place. Now I was completely horrified by it. It was like night of the living dead. I knew that if I didn't get out of the place really quickly they were going to eat my brains just like they had done to my best friend Steve.

If you've ever seen George Lucas' 1971 feature-length film called "thx1138" then you'll have a good visual about what Synanon was like. Most of the extras with shaved heads in the film were recruited from Synanon.

The rules at Synanon were pretty simple: Do what you're told. Speak when spoken to. Submit yourself to attack game therapy and give up all hope of having a normal life. "If this is the only alternative to living life as a drug addict" I thought "I'd rather take my chances on the streets." Come to think of it, if Synanon was the only alternative to death, I think death would've been the preferable option.

By that evening I had found out way more about what was going on in the place than I ever cared to know. The first thing I learned was that an edict had come down from on high that all couples - married or otherwise - had been ordered to separate and find new partners. What the hell this had to do with being a recovering drug addict I'll never know. Another thing that was running through the Synanon grapevine was that the higher ups in the organization were not required to follow any of the rules that the general community members were required to follow. I also learned that many of the top people in the organization had been supplied with brand-new cars and were spending lavish amounts of money partying and drinking.

This was confirmed for me a night or two later when I was crossing the main parking lot in the wee hours of the morning after coming out of a later than usual cleaning session in the kitchen.

I had just emerged from the kitchen building and was headed back toward my room when I noticed someone attempting to park a very fancy foreign convertible and doing a very bad job of it. When the driver finally emerged from the car I recognized him to be one of the higher-ups in the organization. By the way he walked it was quite obvious that he was loaded.

I don't know about anybody else but I have a pretty accurate bull shit meter and it was starting to go off like a fire alarm.

Aside from the fact that the place was showing itself to be a totally bogus scene, the most traumatic experience for me was when they shaved off my nearly waist length hair. The reason it was so traumatic was because my identity was completely wrapped up in being a member of the counterculture and having really long hair was a sort of badge I wore that signified that I was a member of it. When they shaved my head they not only took away my badge, they took away my identity as well. I probably needed a new one anyway.

About a week after my arrival I was sitting in the main lobby staring out the huge plate-glass window that overlooked the ocean. I was contemplating my future life as a zombie when a couple local surfers paddled out and started catching some nice chest to shoulder high waves right behind the building. The site of the two surfers awoke in me an overwhelming longing for freedom. Ever since I was a little kid surfing had been an obsession with me. It was my first love. For me, surfing represented freedom from all the mindless soul stealing garbage that our culture - and Western society as a whole - was attempting to shove down our throats.

It suddenly became very clear that I had to get out and I had to get out now!

Without a second thought I got up and walked down the back stairs to the beach. Without looking back I began to walk up the coast towards Topanga Canyon and freedom.

Fearing they might have sent someone out to bring me back I stuck to the beach as closely as possible, all the while looking over my shoulder. By the time I got to the Gladstone's parking lot at Sunset and PCH I was pretty worn out and decided to take a chance on hitchhiking. By the time I got to Topanga Canyon and PCH I was starting to feel a bit safer though I was pretty sure that my bald head made me stick out like a sore thumb.

On my way up the canyon I hitched a ride with a couple long-haired freaks who - after hearing my story - offered me a place to stay.

The next morning my rescuers supplied me with a bandanna to tie around my head, a battered Fedora, an old beat up fringe jacket and graciously drove me up to the intersection of the 101 and Topanga Canyon where I stuck out my thumb and headed back home to San Francisco.

Chapter 29

Because I had done it so many times before, the trip back up the coast wasn't too bad. I hitchhiked north to my usual spot just outside of Santa Barbara, where I hopped a freight train that took me up near the Watsonville - Salinas area. There I jumped off and thumbed my way back into the City.

I had been gone just a couple of days shy of two months when I got back to San Francisco. Things were pretty much the same at the Fell Street house except that someone else was now living in my room. This wasn't too surprising since it seemed to everyone that I was a goner. I didn't blame them really. I thought I was a goner as well.

Joanne was really glad to see me though her new roommate looked a bit nervous about my return. Fortunately it turned out to be a nonissue because my room was still waiting for me at the Noe street house.

Another bit of good news was that James was out of jail and it looked like they were going to drop most of the charges. And Big Brother was back together working on some new material with Nick Gravenites and Kathy McDonald.

The most surprising thing for me personally was that no one made fun of my lack of hair. I was so self-conscious about it yet no one said a word. The only mention of it came when Paula handed me a beautiful old gray Royal deluxe Stetson and said "You're probably going to need this to keep your head from freezing".

A couple weeks after I got back my friend Robert - who I lived in the tipi with up at Olompali - showed up at the house looking like he had something very serious on his mind. It turned out that he was pretty heavily involved with members of the American Indian Movement (AIM) who had recently taken over Alcatraz Island.

He said that a couple of the leaders of the occupation group had snuck off the island to get supplies and that the FBI had gotten wind of it and had put a dragnet out for them. He sat there looking nervous for a couple minutes and then asked us if we would be willing to put them up until the heat blew over. Paula broke out in a huge grin and nodded her head and I started laughing and looked at Robert and said "What were you so nervous about? Did you actually think that we would say no?" He shook his head and started laughing as well.

I told him that they could have my room for as long as they needed it and Paula said that I could either sleep with her or on the couch in her room if I wanted. A few minutes later Robert went off to gather the troops.

They ended up staying with us for about eight or nine days. We very rarely saw any of them except once or twice late at night when they would come out to use the kitchen or the bathroom. Even then they almost never spoke to us. Other than that, they kept the curtains drawn and the door closed at all times. Then late one night Robert showed up and hustled them all into a car and drove off into the night. I never saw my friend Robert again though I did see a couple of the other guys on the news a few years later at a place called Wounded Knee.

Not long after all the guys in Big Brother - James, Sam, Peter, David - myself and a few other friends went to Janis' house in Larkspur

146

for a party. She was having it as a sort of celebration as she was about to go down to L.A. to finish up her new album.

On the way up to the party James pulled out a bag containing 2 or 3 oz. of cocaine (his drug of choice ever since Nancy died) and asked if we wanted any. Cocaine was still a fairly rare commodity on the scene so I was surprised to see that he had so much of it on him.

I don't remember a lot of what went on or who was there because Janis and I and a dealer friend of ours named Thaddeus spent most of the night going in and out the bathroom of her bedroom suite, doing 'Speedballs' (a combined shot of heroin and cocaine).

My last semi coherent memory was of coming out of the bath room with Janis and going to the kitchen/living room. As we were standing there she leaned up against the wall where all the light switches were and nodded out, slid down the wall and inadvertently turned off all the lights.

I guess it was the lights suddenly going out that brought her out of her nod. When she noticed the place was completely dark she started yelling "Who turned off the fucking lights man?" Since I was still standing right next to her I put my arm behind her and flipped all the switches back up. She gave me a dirty look like it was somehow my fault and walked back towards the bedroom. I don't remember much after that.

A few days later she was dead. News of her death sent shock waves through the community. I remember how people kept saying she was clean at the time she died. Some of them even thought she had been murdered because they knew she had quit doing drugs and couldn't possibly have OD'd. I guess none of them were at that party.

Things began to change very rapidly after that. Paula decided she'd had enough and moved out of Noe Street. The house that James Gurley and Richard Hudgins lived in, was taken over by an amazing group of gender bending theatrical performers - that my friend Fayette Hauser was involved with - called the Cockettes.

Cocketes Fayette
Photo Credit - Clay Geerdes

And I - who was once again strung out - moved into the It's a Beautiful Day band house up near the top of Castro Street, with Val Fuentes, Mitchell Holman, Freddie Web and Patty Santos.

Not wanting to get back into the whole dealing heroin thing, I decided to kick cold turkey as soon as I moved in. I'd been through it quite a few times before so I knew what to expect.

This time however, I got way sicker than usual. Aside from the usual sweating, nausea and cold chills, my whole body ached all over especially my kidneys. A couple days later Val looked in to check on me and said "I think you better go into the bath-room and take a look at your eyes".

When I finally got to the mirror, I was horrified to find that the whites of my eyes were now bright yellow and my skin had turned a greenish yellow. "Great" I thought, "Just what I need, hepatitis". No wonder my urine was such a weird color. Fuck! Now what?

Val and Freddie bundled me in a blanket, stuffed me into the back of the Volkswagen and headed for the emergency room at San Francisco General Hospital.

When they eventually got around to seeing me, I was undressed, pinched, prodded, probed, abandoned, rediscovered, re-examined, diagnosed with serum hepatitis, given a series of shots, a hospital gown and finally admitted.

Several days later, my eyes were no longer yellow and my urine had returned to a normal color. I was feeling much better and I had lots of energy yet for some reason they would not release me so I could go home.

A week and a half later - after having found where they had hidden my clothes - I dressed myself and snuck out the window of my hospital room at about three o'clock in the morning.

Chapter 30

Soon after my ignominious departure through the window of my room at San Francisco General Hospital I began to make regular trips to the Haight-Ashbury free medical clinic detox unit.

What initially started out as an attempt to keep myself from be coming too strung out again, eventually morphed into becoming a full-time voluntary staff member and counselor.

As I began using more and more heroin in an attempt to block out the fact that I was using too much heroin already, it became clear to me that I didn't like the stuff. In fact I hated it. Aside from keeping me from getting sick, all it did was make my face itch and put me in a really funky mood.

"The Clinic", as we came to call it was the first of its kind. It was the brainchild of the couple very cool, very hip young doctors named David Smith and George "Skip" Gay. The place was a strictly supervised outpatient drug treatment program that dispensed free medication to anyone trying to get off drugs.

Aside from the on-site doctors and the resident pharmacologist - Darrell Inaba - the majority of employees and counselors were either college grads with some drug experience or ex-drug addicts from the community.

There was also a statistics department that occupied the top floor run by John Newmeyer (brother of actress Julie Newmar) and of course the free medical health clinic across the street on the corner of Haight and Clayton.

If you consider the amount of drugs that were being used around the nation, it's quite astonishing to find that there were very few places in existence that were capable of dealing with the looming problem of drug addiction.

In most parts of the country, drug addiction was treated as a form of criminal behavior caused by mental illness, with addicts being committed to mental institutions or prisons for varying lengths of time.

The Federal Medical Center at Lexington Kentucky was a prison that managed to combine both forms of institution into one - with the most common drug of abuse for those sent there being heroin and/or morphine.

The only other places available to help addicts at that time were the fl edgling Narcotics Anonymous and the rapidly self transforming looney farm that called itself Synanon.

The Haight-Ashbury free medical clinic detox unit was the first of its kind and quickly became the model for almost all outpatient drug treatment programs that followed. At the time that I became a full fledged volunteer, I lived in a flat that was right next door to the clinic. My first job was to work the intake desk answering phones, handing out intake forms to new patients, retrieving the medical files of the patients who were there for their appointments and handling the urine samples that were randomly required of all patients (nice!).

My duties were soon expanded when I became a member of what we called the "OD Team". The OD team was formed as a response to the mounting number of preventable deaths due to drug overdose, caused by the citywide law that required all hospitals to notify law enforcement agencies in case of suspected drug overdose.

This led many people suffering from drug overdoses to be left on street corners or various other places by their friends who didn't want to be arrested by the police - who either arrived with the medical response team or followed closely on their heels.

Because of the way the clinic was set up Dr. Skip Gay found a loophole in the law that allowed us to respond to cases of suspected drug overdose without the need to notify law enforcement.

Fliers announcing our services along with our hotline number were posted up throughout the community and it wasn't long before we started receiving our first calls.

The teams usually consisted of three staff members and one medical doctor who were on call 24 hours a day, with our response vehicle usually being Skip's Volkswagen beetle. In the short history of the OD team we never lost a single patient. Fortunately, the city of San Francisco realized the problems that the mandatory notification law was causing and shortly afterwards rescinded it.

As things began to get busier with the rapid introduction of heroin into the neighborhood, I started training as a counselor. Shortly afterwards I moved into the huge mansion - turned apartment building - on the corner of Fell and Lyon Street that housed many of the staff members from the clinic.

The staff doctors in the early days were David Smith, Skip Gay, Irving klompus and Craig Whitehead. The criterion for being a drug counselor back then was very different from what it is today. There was no such thing as being a certified detox counselor. Quite simply this was because there was no one to certify you. Not only that -until we came along - there was no one who specialized in the medical treatment of drug addiction that had any firsthand experience of what it was like to be a drug addict.

Haight Detox
Photo Credit - Toni Drew

The biggest problem we had was trying to find a way to help keep the addicts off drugs once they were detoxed. We simply did not have a place to point them towards when they were clean - out patient or otherwise. There was nothing available to us at the time.

Narcotics Anonymous quite new and unknown. Reality House West was a basement flat filled with bare mattresses that resembled a crash pad more than a drug treatment program.

Synanon had become a cult deprogrammers dream and the Salvation Army was just not an option for most of the people in the community. So basically, the clinic became a sort of treadmill, with patients getting clean, going back into the community, getting strung out again, resurfacing as patients at the clinic, getting clean and going back into the community and so on and so forth. Every once in a while though someone would get clean and stay clean, which gave us all hope because the outlook for the future of someone using hard drugs was always pretty grim. The axiom at the time was "Once a junkie, always a junkie" which of course we now know is total bullshit. But that's what people believed.

Late in 1970 we expanded the scope of the detox program to include the use of acupuncture when Skip and David were allowed to bring in 2 traditional acupuncturists from China which they set up in a small storefront around the corner from the detox clinic up on Haight Street.

The unit's success rate was far beyond what any of us expected it to be. A fact I can personally attest to, because at the end of one of my periodic bouts of self-induced drug lunacy, David asked me to forgo the usual round of medications and had me report to the acupuncture clinic instead.

To say I was skeptical is a gross understatement. I wouldn't have gone at all if they hadn't of told me that they needed firsthand information about the efficacy of the project. So I drug my ass out of bed and reported to the unmarked storefront on Haight Street where I placed myself in the hands of two Chinese witch doctors who began sticking needles in me like I was some sort of a voodoo doll.

To my great surprise I became so relaxed that I dozed off on the table I was lying on and slept for almost 2 hours. I say to my great surprise because, as any good junkie will tell you, it is almost impossible to get any sleep when you're kicking dope. "Wow! This shit really works!" I kept saying over and over again in disbelief. What's up with that?

Chapter 31

In an attempt to get the beautiful Fayette Hauser to notice me, I started making regular visits to James Gurley's old house on Oak Street, which was now occupied by the Cockettes.

Inside, the place was a fantasy world of decadent splendor. A kind of sultan's harem on acid where one instantly lost track of time and the boundary lines between day and night, male and female, illusion and reality. The place was a constant beehive of activity populated by the most outrageously flamboyant, amazingly talented group of gender bending freaks ever gathered at one place on the face of the earth. It was like an Aubrey Beardsley painting brought to life by Frederico Fellini! In a word, it was totally insane!

It was there that I first met a young talented singer named Sylvester - who regularly worked as a Billie holiday impersonator - and a group of extremely talented young girls from Oakland that sang with him called the Pointer Sisters. It was through Fayette and the rest of the boys and girls that I met John Waters and Divine who came to live with them a short time later.

The Cockettes were originally founded by a young man who went by the name "Hibiscus", who was a member of a commune called KaliFlower - a freeform arts community that was dedicated to distributing free food and to creating free art and theater.

The Cockettes were a flamboyant ensemble of gay and straight hippies decked out in gender-bending drag with tons of glitter and makeup who performed a series of legendary musicals at The Nocturnal Dream Shows - a weekly midnight eclectic film series put on by underground film director Stephen Arnold's close friend and fellow film director Sabastian at the Palace Theater in North Beach.

With titles like *"Tinsel Tarts in a Hot Coma"*, *"Journey to the Center of Uranus"*, *"Pearls Over Shanghai"*, and *"Hot Greeks"* their performances were always fun and needless to say, way over the top. These all singing, all dancing extravaganzas featured elaborate costumes, rebellious sexuality, and exuberant chaos. By today's standards, it's almost impossible to believe that anything so outrageously funny and creative could have occurred in such an uncalculated, spontaneous manner.

L-R, Pristine Condition, Marshall Olds, Bobby Cameron, Danny Isley, Link Martin

Photo Credit - Fayette Hauser

I had known most of the Cockettes quite a while before they took over the house on Oak Street and a couple of them were my clients at the clinic. My visits to the house were always an adventure, some of which were more bizarre than others. If Fayette or my some-time girl friend Rachel Greene were there, everything was fine. But if I was there alone, I suddenly became fair game, particularly after Divine moved in.

It's amazing how disconcerting it is to have a 300 lb drag queen trying to put the moves on you. The fi rst thing he ever said to me was "Why don't you come over here and sit on my lap boy?" It would have been funny if he hadn't been serious.

I met Sylvester shortly after he arrived in San Francisco from L.A. and after a lot coercing on his part and the other Cockettes, I consented to play bass for him for a couple gigs.

While everyone thought the reason I didn't want to play with him was because I thought I was too cool, the truth of the matter was that I was scared out of my mind.

Yes, I'd jammed with guys from Big Brother, Santana and the Grate ful Dead, but never on stage. Jamming is very different from having to learn a complete song arrangement. When you jam, all you have to know is what key everybody else is in and then try not to mess things up. With Sylvester I had to learn five or six songs, which was something I'd never had to do before. Fortunately pretty much everything he did was sort of Blues/Gospel based. I got through it ok though I was so nervous that I thought I was going to throw up the whole time.

Chapter 32

On one of my many trips to The Family Dog on The Great Highway, I discovered a really cool little surf shop on Wawona Street run by a cantankerous young surfer/shaper named Bob Wise. At the time, Bob's place was the only surf shop North of Santa Cruz and it served as the hub of the local surfing community.

Walking into a surf shop back in those days was always a bit daunting because of the localized nature of surfing as a whole. Each community had its own breaks, cliques and local shapers and anyone from outside the local group was not welcomed with open arms. It was sort of like a barroom scene from an old Western where everyone stops what they're doing and just stares at the cowboy when he first walks in.

Bob carried wetsuits, surfboards, wax, basically anything and everything a surfer could need. The thing that really caught my eye though was the selection of skateboards that he carried, which consisted mostly of G&S, Makaha and Hobie brand boards.

My original intention was to get a used board and go surfing, which I did. But after nearly freezing to death, drowning and seeing the evidence of a run-in Bob had with a Great White Shark, I decided to forgo the frigid waters of San Francisco and concentrated on skateboarding.

Now as anyone who's been paying attention knows, the true nature of reality is quite synchronous, so I was quite pleased when I found a pair of used shoe skates with weird translucent green wheels made by Sure Grip a couple days after buying a G&S fibreflex from Bob.

I took my find along with the deck I'd just purchased back to Bob who helped me switch the wheels out. I immediately took the board out for a test ride and was amazed at how smooth and quiet the board was. It turned out the wheels were made of something called polyurethane - a substance invented in 1937 by the German company I.G Farben, the same company that brought us such wonderful products as: Zyklon-B and Heroin. Heroin being marketed under the company's subsidiary name of 'Bayer' - the aspirin folks.

While they were way better than composition wheels, they didn't grip nearly as well as the early Cadillac and Road Rider wheels that became available 3 or 4 years later.

Terry Nails & friend, Haight St
1970 Photo Credit - Esquire

Chapter 33

During this whole period I was still working at the clinic three to five days a week. Unfortunately, being a drug counselor at that time was not a guarantee that you would or even could stay clean more successfully than anyone else and I once again fell off into the bag pretty hard. Skip and Daryl did the best they could to keep me on the straight and narrow, all to no avail.

By the end of November I'd fi nally had enough. Realizing that I would never get away from the stuff as long as I stayed in the city, I loaded my pockets up with a couple week's worth of meds and headed up to the Russian River with my old girlfriend Saffron.

We rented a small cabin in a beautiful area everybody jokingly referred to as "The ghetto in the Redwoods" Rio Nido. The cabin had been one of several that had originally served as weekend resort/motor court rentals in the 1940s.

Because of a series of periodic floods that ravaged the area, business had declined over the last few years and the cabins were now rented out on a long-term basis for $50 a month. That may sound cheap but you have to remember that in San Francisco you could rent a five-bedroom Victorian flat for between $35 and $75 a month.

The cabin was constructed of uninsulated Redwood with all the inner studs and beams exposed on the interior. It had a large main living area/bedroom with a separate small kitchen and bathroom. It had all the makings of a place that one could quietly freeze to death in during the winter except for the fact that it had an incredibly well functioning gas heater that even on the coldest days, could make the place unbearably hot if you weren't paying attention.

It took me about five days to go through all two weeks' worth of meds I brought with me. About an hour after I took my last Darvon-N I went into typical junkie panic mode and started casting around to see if I could find a place to cop some dope. (Some Horse! Some Horse! My kingdom for some Horse!)

Talking about getting clean is one thing, but actually doing it is quite another or so I'm told. The truth of the matter is that kicking dope is really no big deal. Hell, I've been way sicker with the flu and food poisoning than I ever was kicking heroin. It's the mental/psychological part that's actually tougher to get through than the withdrawal symptoms.

The reason for this has to do with brain chemistry. In particular it's how the brain functions while on heroin that causes the feelings of desperation and panic that arise once the substance is out of the neurological system.

To quote an article published in *Philosophical Transactions of the Royal Society, Biological Sciences*, titled *Neural Mechanisms Underlying the Vulnerability to develop Compulsive Drug Seeking Habits and Addiction:*

"We describe evidence that the switch from controlled to compulsive drug seeking represents a transition at the neural level from prefrontal cortical to striatal control over drug-seeking and drug-taking behaviors as well as a progression from ventral to more dorsal domains of the striatum, mediated by its serially interconnecting dopaminergic

circuitry. These neural transitions depend upon the neuroplasticity induced by chronic self-administration of drugs in both cortical and striatal structures, including long-lasting changes that are the conse-quence of toxic drug effects. " (Memorize that. There will be a test on it later.)

To put it in layman's terms, the brain rewires the way it processes dopamine and consequently many of the associated neural pathways while under the influence of prolonged opiate use. Fortunately, this process is reversible, unlike the effects some of the other drugs like methamphetamine and cocaine have on the neural structure.

Anyway… A few days later I was feeling fine and ready for action. The main stumbling block on my road to staying clean was that I had to be in the city on the 1st and 15th of every month to cash my dole checks which were now my only source of income. The problem wasn't getting to the city. That part was pretty easy. The problem was getting out of the city and back to the river without spending all the money on dope.

Thankfully, Saffron found someone with a car and she volunteered to pick up my check for me while she was down picking up hers. I started getting worried when Saffron's ride returned without her later that day. When I asked where she was the neighbor who gave her a ride told me that her check hadn't arrived yet and she decided to stay down there and wait for it. When she finally returned three days later with my check she was so fucked up on heroin that I was afraid to even let her sit down for fear that she might pass out and stop breathing.

I don't know if I was more pissed off at her for taking so long to come back or for getting loaded without me. The same thing happened again two weeks later.

After about a month I felt strong enough to be able to go in and pick up my checks without buying any dope. My mission was made a lot easier because I spent my entire time in the city hanging out with Skip, Sunshine, Mike Bachel, Skeezics, Mary Sue, Wild Bill,

Jim Singleton, Daryl and the rest of the crew that I had worked with at the Clinic.

By the beginning of January Saffron had moved out and gotten her own place a couple of miles down the road in Guernwood and I had the place all to myself, sort of. Actually, I had a new 4 legged roommate. The story goes something like this:

A month or so earlier Saffron had returned from one of her forays into the city with the biggest, most beautiful, frighteningly intelligent Collie ever to grace the face of the earth. From what I can understand Saffron met a young couple in the city who were in the process of moving out of San Francisco and into a small apart-ment in New York City. This young couple had a Collie named Baron that they were desperately trying to fi nd a good home for. When they found out that Saffron lived out in the country on the Russian River they literally begged her to take Baron with her.

It really was quite eerie how alert and intelligent Baron was. He always seemed to be in complete command of any situation that arose. We never once had to direct any of his movements or scold him for anything whatsoever. He always seemed to know exactly what to do.

The next morning after he arrived, I decided to take him for a walk down along the 116 towards Guerneville. There was usually very little traffic on the road at that time a year, but I was still a bit concerned for Baron's safety. It was quite foggy on the road and we walked about half a mile without seeing a single car. Baron all the while had been running around checking everything out. I lost track of him for a few minutes and started to become concerned when from out of nowhere, he appeared at my side and started nudging me off the side of the road. A few seconds later a car came zooming past us out of the fog. As soon as it had passed Baron once again took off on his adventure, only to return to herd me off the side of the road the next time he heard a car coming.

On another morning, I heard a dog related commotion outside and got up to see what was going on.

The source of the commotion turned out to be the neighborhood bully dog, from down the road, attacking my neighbor's cute little toy poodle named Lisa. I got to the front door just in time to see Baron grab the dog from down the road by the back of the neck and throw him about 4 feet straight up in the air. The dog turned snarling and baring his teeth at Baron who just stood there silently staring at him. A couple seconds later the dog took off running as fast as he could. We never saw him in our area again. His actions were so far beyond those of a normal dog that people were always coming up to me and saying things like "You know that's not a dog don't you?" I would just smile and nod my head. Personally, I figured he was either an enlightened master who had purposely reincarnated in the form of a dog or he was a shape shifting wizard. In any case, no matter what any of us thought, the one incontrovertible fact was that he was amazing.

Not long after Saffron moved out I was awakened in the wee dawn hours of the morning by someone knocking on my door. I opened it to find my friend Jodi Marcos - an unbelievably beautiful girl from the Philippines - accompanied by a very thin, very pale young guy with longhair, a beard and a heavy British accent. She told me her friend's name was Paul, we shook hands and I invited them in. I seated them on the couch and asked if they wanted any tea as I headed towards the kitchen.

After putting the kettle on, I rejoined them in the main room, at which point Jodi's friend looked at me and said "Have you got a fag?" I don't know whether it was because I was so groggy or that his accent was so heavy, but I thought he was asking me if I was a fag.

I just stared at him sort of dumbfounded with my mouth open trying to figure out what the hell was going on. When he finally realized I didn't understand what he had said, he held up two fi ngers in front of his mouth and said "A fag, you know, a ciggie" at which point my brain started the function again. "Oh you mean a cigarette, sure" I said and we both busted out laughing.

Jodi told me that she had met Paul at the Fillmore and had decided to give him a tour of the Russian River. She suddenly got all excited and asked him if she could tell me what band he was in. He looked pretty apprehensive at first and finally nodded his head in agreement. With a big grin on her face Jodi told me that he was the lead singer in a band called 'Free'.

Having never heard of them before I nodded my head and said "Cool, what kind of music do you guys do?" Realizing that I had no idea who he or the band was, the guy immediately relaxed and told me they did a sort of bluesy rock. He then asked if he could see my guitar and started showing me some new stuff he had been working on. I then showed him some stuff that I've been working on. Not long after he stepped out of the cabin and returned with a beautiful old Gibson acoustic guitar.

By the time we were done jamming it was nearly dark. Jodi said she had to get back to the city to take care of some business, but that she'd be back in a couple days. Paul looked disappointed with the idea of having to go back. I told him that he was welcome to stay as long as he liked. He stayed for quite a while…

Paul fit in pretty well with our ragtag group of cabin dwellers. The group consisted of Gary and Cathy Jones and their two kids - who lived at the top of the road on the right - Craig and Michelle and their toy poodle Lisa - lived right next door to them - Jason, Joe and Buzzy who lived two cabins up from me on the left and two big beautiful blonde girls from Sweden that we called the chocolate cake sisters -because of their obsession with baking cakes and cooking - who lived right across the road from me.

Paul and I fell into a routine of taking Baron for long walks in the mornings until we realized it was much more fun if we let him take us for walks instead.

As spring approached Baron's morning adventure walks would sometimes turn into all-day fishing expeditions. The rest of the days though were almost always taken up sitting around playing music except for those occasions when we would hitchhike into the city.

One day an emergency situation arose in which we needed to find a car fast in order to get one of the kids to a doctor. Paul miraculously produced a pair of keys and with a sort of embarrassed look on his face led us down to a car that he had stashed in the trees down near the entrance to the cabin area. It turned out that his record company had supplied him with a car which he wanted nothing to do with. He preferred to live the way we did and do exactly the same things that we did every day which included hitchhiking when necessary.

We all thought it was pretty funny and a couple of days later he and I drove to the city to return the car and hitchhiked back to the river.

Near the end of January Paul told us he had a gig at the Santa Monica Civic in LA and asked if we would come with him to the gig. We said we'd love to but we didn't think we could afford the gas which Paul immediately offered to pay for.

Paul wearing shirt I gave him Best-Of-Free album cover
Photo Credit - A&M Records

The next day Paul, Saffron, Baron and I hitchhiked into the city to pick up some money and supplies for the trip. On our way back later that afternoon we got stuck hitchhiking near the entrance of the Sausalito houseboat community called Gate Six. During a lull in the traffic, Baron and Paul went over to investigate the flood control ditch that ran alongside the highway when all of a sudden the embankment gave way and both Paul and Baron went tumbling into the black muddy water below. A couple of seconds later, Baron came scrambling up the embankment soaking wet and completely covered with black mud, closely followed by Paul who was in a similar condition and laughing his ass off.

Baron immediately started shaking the mud and water off of himself, covering Paul with even more mud, which made him laugh even harder.

In the meantime, a guy who had seen us hitchhiking and circled back around to pick us up, arrived just in time to see the comedy of errors play itself out in full. The driver was a guy I'd met before who lived in a little town near the river called Forestville. Taking pity on the soaking wet, mud covered Paul and the slightly less mud covered Baron, he graciously offered to drive us all the way to Rio Nido.

A few days later Paul and I packed our guitars, sleeping bags, and clothing into the back of Craig and Michelle's temperamental 1953 Mercury station wagon - named Otis - and the four of us headed for LA.

Otis ran like a champ the whole way and we arrived in LA about 10 hours later, checking into the room that had been reserved for Paul about 11 o'clock that night.

The next morning we were woken up by a very funny, scruffy looking little guy with a huge mane of hair that turned out to be the band's guitar player Paul Kossoff. A few minutes later we were joined by another young gentleman named Simon Kirk. With Craig and Michelle already occupying the bathroom, I went down the hall with the young guitar player to use the one in his room. The guy was absolutely delightful, with a sense a humor that reminded me of Keith Moon without the accompanying maniacal behavior.

We all piled into Otis and took off to find a good place to eat breakfast after which we spent the rest of the day cruising around Santa Monica and hanging out at the beach.

We got back to the hotel at about 3:30 in the afternoon at which point Paul took off and I decided to take a nap. Shortly afterwards I was awakened by the return of Paul who looked very disheveled and emotionally distraught. He said he didn't feel like talking so we went for a walk on the beach. After a while he began telling me how he and the bass player, Andy Fraser, were constantly getting into arguments. He said that the arguments had become so bad lately, that they would occasionally erupt into fist fights.

When we got back to the room, Paul looked like he needed some rest so I grabbed my guitar and headed down the Kossoff's room. There Koss and I and Simon spent most of the night jamming and drinking wine while I regaled them with stories of the Haight-Ashbury and country life on the Russian River.

I woke up the next morning on the floor of Kossoff's room with a headache the size of Texas and a taste in my mouth that would've embarrassed the Ravenous Bugblatter Beast of Traal (look it up).

I drug myself off the floor and out the door and immediately began begging anyone that I saw for aspirins. Fortunately a kindly house-maid took pity on my lowly personage and bestowed several tablets of the sought after substance on my humbled self.

I then went back to the room to take a shower and try to put the pieces of my brain back together before we all went out to breakfast.

After we ate, Paul, Craig and Michelle decided to try and do a little more sightseeing before three o'clock when we had to be at the Civic for sound check. I, on the other hand, elected to stay at the hotel and feel sorry for my head and await their return. Kossoff popped in to check on me a few minutes after I got back and we ended up spending the rest of the afternoon telling stories. At one point he started asking me questions about different kinds of drugs, and expressed a particular interest in heroin. I had already told him about the problems I'd had with the stuff so I told him "Here's the deal, stay the fuck away from that shit. Don't even think about it. If you do it even once and you like it, you'll be fucked for the rest of your life. Believe me, it ain't worth it."

Unfortunately, he didn't heed my warning and I was greatly saddened when I learned of the fatal overdose he suffered on a plane trip back to England five years later.

At three o'clock on the dot a black limo showed up to pick the guys up and take them to sound check. Paul seemed to be appalled at the idea of riding in a limo and opted instead to make the trip in Otis. Having grown used to moving equipment around I jumped in to lend a hand whenever it was needed.

The sound check went pretty well considering the boomy sounding acoustics of the place. Afterwards we all wandered off together to check out downtown Santa Monica and get something to eat before show time.

Just before the guys went on, Paul pulled out a large plastic bag containing the muddy clothes he was wearing when he fell in the ditch in Sausalito and put them on before going out on stage to sing. He had a big grin on his face as he passed me and I followed him out laughing my ass off.

The set was great though the crowd kept yelling for them to turn it up which they eventually did.

In order to avoid the after show hangers on, Paul, Craig, Michelle and I headed straight back to the hotel the minute they were done playing.

Bright and early the next morning we packed up Otis and all four of us headed back to the Russian River, with the other band members opting to take off for Mexico instead.

Paul spent the next few weeks with us hanging out at the cabins, exploring the nearby coast and searching for Hot Springs until it was time to go back on tour again.

We didn't see a whole lot of him after that, though he did reappear a couple more times to spend a few days with us.

As the summer went on the band began a tour overseas and a couple months later we all moved out of the cabins and into an 18 room mansion that our friend Mary Black had rented which was located on Canyon Road 2 a short ways down the road.

I did hook up with Paul a couple times over the next few years, but the youthful innocence of those early days had seemingly passed both of us by, though we did have a couple of more adventures. But that, as they say in the fairytale books, is another story…

Chapter 34

The mansion that our friend Mary Black had rented was actually an old resort Lodge made out of solid redwood that had 18 bedrooms, each of which had its own bathroom.

The bedrooms were arranged on two different levels with the upper-level rooms being accessed by a balcony style walkway that overlooked a huge high ceiling central ballroom. At the far end of the ballroom stood a huge walk in fireplace.

Mary had rented the entire place for $150 a month and immediately set about gathering up all of her friends and offering them these huge beautiful rooms for $20 a month.

Barron, however, didn't seem to like the crowds and took off to go live with Saffron, though he did come back to visit from time to time. My friend Claude Palmer came to live with us and he quickly found himself playing in a local band called Squeeze (no, not the one from England) and another project with Gary Jones on guitar, his wife Kathy on bass, our friend Buzzy on drums and occasionally, myself. We were called the Hot Water blues band.

It wasn't long before the ballroom area turned into a rehearsal studio and it quickly became known as a place to jam by everyone passing through the Russian River area.

About three months after we moved in, the local sheriff paid us a visit saying that one of the neighbors had called and told him that there was a bucket of blood sitting in the old carriage house beneath the building. It seems the caller thought that we might be some sort of a Charles Manson type cult.

Being quite curious about the whole thing ourselves, eight or so of us trooped down around the back of the building with the Sheriff and stood by as he opened up the half rotted creaky doorway that led into the carriage area.

Sure enough, sitting off to one side near the center of the room was a bucket filled with a very suspicious looking dark red substance that on closer inspection turned out to be redwood stain. The sheriff left with a big smile on his face shaking his head and we all had a pretty good laugh about the whole thing.

If you consider the amount of people who lived there - all of whom had friends who were constantly dropping by - and add in the now nearly 24-hour a day jam sessions that were happening, you'll get a pretty good idea of just how hectic the place could be at times.

One morning, I walked outside to find a couple of nearly naked, pale skinned Scottish lads named Robin Williamson and Mike Heron from The Incredible String Band sitting on our front steps.

They told me they'd heard the music and wanted to know if they could come in and check it out. They came in and jammed with us for a couple hours before heading back up the canyon to the house where they were staying. They both returned a couple more times over the next week or so, with Mike Heron returning a few times by himself after Robin had left to go back to Scotland.

Because of the amount of commotion that was going on at the house I began to spend more time at Saffron's hanging out with her and Baron.

Things went pretty well at Saffron's until I received a letter from a friend of mine stationed in Vietnam containing four bags of Vietnamese heroin.

The accompanying letter stated that each bag cost 2 American dollars and contained about a quarter of a Gram of white powder. The letter also very specifically stated that I was to do no more than a match head size amount of it at a time. As it turned out, a match head was way too much. I found this out the hard way when I woke up hanging over the rail of the balcony, being slapped in the face with an ice cold towel and a bag full of ice stuffed down the front of my pants.

Believe it or not, in all the years that I messed around with that crap, that was the first and only time that I ever OD. Of course it only takes one time to kill you - a fact my little brother Ted also found out the hard way a few years later...

"All things are impermanent" the Buddha once said and so it was with the mansion in the redwoods. The place was sold and we all had to move out bringing to a close a very fun and very interesting unintentional experiment in communal living.

Claude, Gary, Kathy and the little ones, Buzzy, Wade, and I all moved into an abandoned barroom at a place called Aries Corner and started working on material for the band. We did a few gigs around the area with the most memorable one being a birthday party we played for the sculptor, artist, dancer and L.A. "freak scene" guru, Vito Paulekas. During the last part of the set legendary producer Kim Fowley got up and did a song with us during which he spit out his false teeth, threw himself off the stage and proceeded to roll around in the dirt. A good time was had by all.

As with the mansion, this too came to an end when the place was put on the market and I soon found myself back in the city working at the clinic.

Chapter 35

Things had changed a bit since I last worked there, with the addition of the new child services department located down the street and several new employees, one of which was a cute little redhead named Toni Drew, who for some reason, I just couldn't seem to keep my hands off of.

I initially tried to make a go of it with my old girlfriend Rachel Greene, but shortly after we got back together we met a couple from Los Angeles named Nick and Deborah, the result being that Rachel took off with Nick and Deborah and I ended up together by default.

It was sort of fun at first, but Deborah had one major flaw as far as I was concerned. She was extremely rich, very spoiled, and was used to getting anything she wanted.

A week or so after we got together, she presented me with the keys to a beautiful 1962 3.8 Jaguar. This would've been a really nice gift if that was in fact what it was supposed to be. But I don't think she ever did anything without having an ulterior motive. It didn't take me long to realize that there were a lot of strings attached to that car and I tried to give her the keys back a couple of weeks later. She refused to take them and promised to stop trying to manipulate me but was unable to keep her promise. I slipped the keys into her purse a short time later and never drove the car again.

I had already stopped seeing her more than once or twice a week and was on the verge of calling it off completely when fate reared its ugly head and I found myself in a situation where it was very useful to have a rich girlfriend.

Debra had gone back to LA and taken the Jaguar with her. I was back to living at the Lion Street house and hanging out with Toni, the cute little redhead from the clinic. Things were going pretty well and I was staying clean for the most part when the shit hit the fan.

What happened was this: One of my clients at the clinic that the entire staff had taken a great interest in had suddenly disappeared. The client was the female dope dealer Trina who had all the kids. She had been coming to see me every day like clockwork for the last three weeks and had tested negative for opiates the entire time. Her skin had cleared up, her eyes were bright and she was happier than we had ever seen her and then she just disappeared.

A couple days later when she still hadn't shown up, Skip, Daryl and I had a little meeting. It was decided that it might be a good idea if somebody went over to check on her and see if everything was okay. So on my way back to the Lion Street house after work that night I dropped by her flat to check on her.

I walked up the stairs, knocked on her front door and the instant the door started to open I was grabbed from behind and thrown headfirst into and through the not quite open-door by a group of plane clothed and uniformed police officers led by Billy Marlow, the former partner of my old nemesis officer Garrett. I had unwittingly walked right into the middle of a bust.

I stood handcuffed against the wall and watched as San Francisco's finest methodically tore the place to shreds. For a while it looked like they may have made a mistake, when from out of nowhere one of the officers produced a bag containing close to an ounce of heroin. For a minute, I thought that they might have planted it. But seeing how pinned Trina's eyes were, and the look on her face when they found it, told me otherwise. I tried to explain to the officers that I was her drug counselor and that I had been sent to check on her by Dr. Skip Gay of the Haight-Ashbury free medical clinic but they didn't want to hear any of it.

I was shoved into the back of a police car, taken down to the city jail, fingerprinted, photographed, stripped naked, inspected and booked for attempting to buy a schedule one narcotic, conspiring to sell a schedule one narcotic and visiting a house of ill repute (whatever the hell that means).

I was dumped into a holding tank until about one in the morning and then transferred to one of the larger units that contained several bunks.

While I had spent quite a bit of time in juvenile facilities, I had no idea what to do in this particular situation. I'd never been in a real jail before. When they told me I was allowed one phone call, I called Debra in LA instead of Skip like I should have.

Debra told me not to worry. She would have me out of the place in no time. Unfortunately, she was more clueless than I was. The most bizarre thing about the whole incident, as I found out later, was that the cops didn't seem to have any idea that I was even in their jail. I had somehow gotten lost in the system. If I hadn't gotten in trouble while I was in there - which is what finally brought me to their attention - I might still be there today!

Deborah flew in from LA and showed up for a visit the next day. She said she was trying to find me a lawyer, but the cops kept telling her that they couldn't find any record of my arrest.

She asked if I needed any money. "Only if I want to eat something besides jail food" I said. When she found out I was only allowed to have $20 a day on the books she somehow talked one of the guards into bringing me in a little bit of extra cash - $500 to be exact.

Things started to get a little bit tense when the guard walked up to the front of the cell, called out my name and counted out $500 worth of $20 bills one by one in front of everyone in the unit. Fortunately the first night I was there I had been befriended by a Jheri curled, well-dressed young pimp/dealer, who seemed to run the place, so the guys left me alone.

Using the jailhouse grapevine my new friend and I managed to buy up every bag of dope, bottle of methadone, book of matches and pack of cigarettes in the place. Eventually we struck up a deal with the medics who started selling shampoo bottles filled with methadone to us directly, which we split up and sold, quadrupling our money.

It was this setup that finally brought me to the attention of the officials when we were caught mid-deal by one of the officers. I was grabbed and searched. I had all my money confiscated along with the remaining methadone. I was then put into a 12 bunk cell all by myself with orders that no one was supposed to talk to me except the officer in charge of the watch while they tried to figure out what to do with me.

The solution was fairly simple really. They couldn't charge me without letting everybody else know that there was some really fishy stuff going on in the city jail. At the same time they didn't think it was wise to let me just walk out on the streets so I was brought into the courtroom where I was told that I could either sign the document in front of me which allowed them to put me on a brand-new experimental methadone on treatment program and go home or they would simply take me back to my cell and throw away the key.

In hindsight, I should have just gone back to my cell; it would've been far easier on me. But I never really didn't care too much for jail. The most idiotic part of the whole episode was that I was completely clean at the time.

Chapter 36

Methadone: a visit to Vajra Hell

Methadone was developed in 1937 in Germany by scientists working for I.G. Farbenindustrie AG at the Farbwerke Hoechst (Yes! the same wonderful folks who invented Zyklon-B, Heroin and Polyurethane) who were looking for a synthetic opioid that could be created with readily available precursors, to solve Germany's opium shortage problem. The reason for its swift abandonment as an alternative to morphine was due to the adverse effects it had on German soldiers during early trials. In contrast to morphine, which was used to alleviate pain in the injured but also to boost the esteem, stamina, and drive of German soldiers in combat, methadone had effects that have been described as such; " Methadone: aka Dolophine (lovingly named after that great humanitarian Adolf "don't call me Schicklegruber" Hitler) had many adverse effects on the soldiers to whom it was given, leading to apathy, lethargy, and decreased willingness to engage in combat".

Vajra hell: not a place but a state of mind. The state of mind where one feels completely cut off from the only positive things that exist in life and having damaged one's own ability to take and keep vows in the future which is a pretty good description of the way methadone makes you feel.

The West side methadone clinic was located in a mostly black neighborhood known as the Western Addition, near the corner of Ellis and Pierce. The Clinic was run by an upper crust young black clinical pharmacologist named Wesley who the brothers were always making fun of. I'm not sure why they were making fun of him. Maybe it was his hand tailored English made suits or possibly the brand-new BMW he drove. Most likely though it was his inability to let loose and talk jive with the rest of the guys. I think he really would have if he had been capable of it, but the truth of the matter was that Wesley was a highly educated nerd who was as stiff as an English Lord! He couldn't have "got down with da' boys" if his life depended on it. Fortunately for him, it didn't.

Methadone maintenance was nothing new. The Veterans Administration had been using it for quite a while to help treat the returning Vietnam vets who had become strung out while overseas. This, however, was the first time that they ever opened the program to the general public.

As with any new endeavor, there are always some inherent problems. Because the program was based on the military model, they had to rely on the information supplied to them by the Veterans Administration regarding dosage. This information, however, turned out to be extremely unhelpful. Rather than researching what the optimal dosage should be, the VA simply kept raising the dosage until the patient quit complaining.

This led to a situation where some of the patients did quite well on the starting dose of 80 - 90 mg while others ended up on almost 250 mg a day. It took almost 2 years for them to figure out that the initial dose of methadone was already too high in all but the most extreme cases. The optimal maintenance dosage nowadays is 35 mg, with the highest dosage being right about 65 mg.

Coming right out of jail and onto an 80 mg plus daily dose of methadone, was really quite an eye-opener or more appropriately an eye closer. By the time I got off the bus on my way home from the clinic I could barely keep my eyes open I was so loaded. It was all I could do to drag myself upstairs into my room where

I would usually nod out until it was time to go to the clinic the next morning.

Within a week or so I was finally able to function enough to go back to work at the clinic and start riding my skateboard again, or so I'm told because I have little memory of it.

Sometime during the first few weeks of my new fog brained existence I became friends with a guy named Bobby who rode the same bus as me to the clinic every morning. He was extremely cool, down to earth, and very personable. I didn't find out till much later that Bobby was the well-known jazz vibes player Bobby Hutcherson - a leader of the post-bop jazz movement who had played with everybody from Herbie Hancock to Dexter Gordon.

Initially our usual conversations consisted of the normal type of chitchat people pass back-and-forth when they're trying to kill time on a bus ride. As time went on we started going out to breakfast or coffee after the clinic, usually accompanied by a jazz bassist named Dahoud Williams. One morning, Bobby told me he was doing a free music workshop later that afternoon at a little jazz club called "The Both And" at 350 Divisadero and invited me to come along with him.

Thinking that the class would be based on jazz improvisation, I was quite surprised when he pulled out the sheet music for Erik Satie's The Gymnopédies - which is still one of my favorite classical piano compositions - and began to play them on the piano. As he played each part he explained the significance of how the mildly dissonant chord structures worked as the perfect counterpoint with the simple melodies. Afterwards he held up the sheet music and pointed out that on each one of the music staffs the notes had been written without the usage of the bar lines that indicate the length of each measure.

I probably learned more that day sitting there watching him than I ever did in all the music classes I took in school as a kid.

After the class I mentioned that I had just purchased an album that had completely blown me away. The album was "Miles Davis: a tribute to Jack Johnson." It was like nothing that I'd ever heard before. It was an avant-garde jazz funk rock fusion type thing that had me mesmerized. I was so impressed with what I heard that I sat down and played it over and over again until I had learned the bass parts on both sides of the album.

Bobby then went over to a little record player in the back and played me the full album track of the theme song from the TV series "Ironsides" by Quincy Jones. Up until that point, I had only heard the TV version which was pretty watered down by comparison. He then played me another track by Quincy called "Killer Joe". I loved both of the tracks and asked him if I could borrow the albums so I could try and learn them.

One morning as I was getting on the bus to head back to the Haight Bobby said "why don't you grab your bass and come down to the club this afternoon around 3:30?" (the club being the Both And). "Sure" I said "what's going on?" "Just a little jam, see ya'…"

All I can say is that I'm so thankful that I had no idea who any of these guys were when I showed up. Hell, I didn't even really know very much about Bobby's background. I came strolling into the club with my bass acting like I actually knew what I was doing. The truth of the matter was that I could hold my own pretty well in a hippie type jam if no one was paying too close of attention.

Bobby introduced me to a trombone player named Julian Priester and a trumpet player whose name totally escapes me, a sax player named Joe and a drummer whose name I believe was Eddie Marshall (though I can't say for sure) and of course our friend Dahoud Williams was there with his standup.

I felt very confident and completely at ease for some reason when I plugged in and began to play - probably a side effect of the massive amounts of methadone I was on.

This feeling lasted for nearly 30 seconds, until I found myself hopelessly lost in a sea of improvisational creativity. I was so lost that I had to stop playing in order to find a place to jump back in. This caused everyone else to stop as well.

Feeling quite embarrassed, I told Bobby that I was having a hard time following the drummer. "That's because you're not supposed to follow the drummer" he said. "In rock the drummer is the anchor point, in jazz it's the bass player."

I just sat there with a sort of stunned look on my face. "Look" he said, "Just play the groove and don't worry about anything that anyone else is doing, including the drummer. Just keep the time signature going and we'll get back to you."

This was easier said than done for someone who had learned to implicitly rely on the drummer to keep things going. It was like learning how to ride a bicycle without training wheels. At first I had to keep count in my head, but after a while I started to get the hang of it. After all, my favorite bass player in the world Jack Cassidy had been the driving center around which all the members of the Jefferson airplane wove their tapestry of sound. Though the members of the airplane never got as far away from him as these guys were sometimes getting away from me.

I barely got through that jam session by the skin of my teeth. I felt like I had let everyone down, though no one said anything to that effect. A couple weeks later Bobby came up to me and told me that he had a gig that night and asked me to come sit in with him. "Are you kidding? No way! You are way out of my league, I don't even know any of the songs" I said. He just laughed and said, "Don't worry, we'll make it up as we go." And that's exactly what we did.

Eventually, the Lyon Street house was sold and we all had to leave. I moved into a house with Toni over near Polk Street. The West-side clinic was closed down and the entire staff and clientele were transferred to a shabby little building on Ivy Street a block and a half away from the Civic Center.

In the meantime, Bobby began recording and touring quite a bit and I soon lost contact with him completely. It wasn't until years later that I realized the honor I was given when he asked me to play with him that night, and for that I will be forever grateful...

Chapter 37

One of the major effects that opiate use has on the psyche is that it lends a sort of fog brained softness to your everyday level of awareness. Things that a normal person would immediately become aware of can go almost completely unnoticed by someone under the influence of opiates. I say almost completely because I finally realized that the green Ford four-door sedan that I had seen at different places in the city every day for almost 2 weeks was an unmarked police car that for some reason seemed to be following me.

The reason for this I found out at six in the morning a couple of days later when I was awakened by a knock on the door. When I opened it I found two very large human beings standing there with police badges and hands. I recognized one of them as the former narcotics officer turned homicide detective, Napoleon Hendrix.

Officer Hendrix had gained a reputation of being a square shooter while he was working in narcotics so when he asked if they could come in and talk to me I immediately gave my consent.

Aside from being a good honest cop, Hendrix was probably the tallest guy on the force standing 6 foot 5 in stocking feet. When he entered the small studio apartment I was staying in he had to duck his head to get through the door.

Hendrix had a way about him that always put whoever he was talking to completely at ease. I was no different. I apologized for the lack of furniture in the small apartment and pointed Officer Hendrix and his partner towards the bed as a place to sit. They both declined my offer and the 6'5" Hendrix took off his coat and sat down cross-legged on the floor. He then began asking me questions about my movements and whereabouts over the last few weeks. I told him that daily routine consisted of an early morning visit to the methadone clinic followed by work at the Haight clinic and not much else.

He then asked me if I knew a guy named Nick something or other and added that I might have known him by his nickname "Found". I told him that he was a friend of mine that I had met when I first got to the Haight and that he had more recently been one of my clients at the clinic.

I asked Officer Hendrix what it was all about and he told me that my friend had been robbed and murdered by having his throat cut. He then added that I was the last person seen with him before he died. He then went on to tell me that they knew that Found had been a heroin dealer and asked me if I knew or had heard of anyone who had been threatening him or anyone else involved in the drug scene. I told him that I had recently heard that the rip-off artist Fast Joey was back on the scene and that his whole MO was based on threatening and robbing drug dealers.

He then stood up, shook my hand and thanked me for the information and he and his partner left. I was so shocked by the news of my friend's murder that it wasn't until several hours later that I realized that I had actually been a suspect in the case.

Have you ever noticed that when the going gets weird, the weir-does start popping up out of the woodwork? Well, as if my involvement with the homicide squad wasn't bizarre enough, a week or so later a very drunk little Middle Eastern guy who had taken a shine to my girlfriend began making phone calls to our house around 3 AM one morning.

After the fourth phone call in a row I told him to stop calling, hung up the phone and unplugged it from the wall. An hour and a half later I was awakened by a pounding on the front door. I opened it to find myself face-to-face with an enraged drunken Middle Easterner pointing a 357 Magnum at me. He raised the gun to my head and began telling me how I had transgressed some ancient Middle Eastern law against hanging up on someone and how death was too good for me.

Realizing that he was just drunk enough to shoot me, I pointed out to him that if he shot me right then and there he was probably going to have to shoot my girlfriend as well. I knew this was something he didn't want to do because of the huge crush he had on her.

I got dressed as quietly as possible and went downstairs with him. I then got into the driver seat of his car and drove around town with him holding a gun to my ribs until he sobered up.

While it may seem that I was handling the situation pretty well the truth of the matter is that I was scared shitless the entire time. When he finally realized how stupid he had been acting he handed me the gun and started crying and hugging me and begging me to forgive him.

We sat and talked for a really long time and he poured his heart out to me about his family and how weird things were back in the old country. After a couple of hours we drove back to the house where he dropped me off and I never saw him again.

Chapter 38

Once I moved out of the Haight, my working days at the clinic became few and far between. After about 5 months I finally stopped going altogether.

The Polk Street area - which had previously been a mostly gay area - was now attracting a more eclectic mix of people with the addition of several women's boutiques and straight businesses like the Head Shop, Mom's Apple Grave and the Palms Cafe.

I had been on the Methadone maintenance program long enough that I now only had to go in one day a week to check in and pickup six take homes. The rest of the week I spent riding my skateboard and hanging out at the Palms and looking for somebody to play music with.

The newest drug of choice in the area was something called Methaqualone which was manufactured under the trademark name Quaalude - though better known as 'Ludes' or disco biscuits on the street. Quaaludes were a hypnotic sedative that had become increasingly popular as a recreational drug in the late 1960s - early 1970s.

Noticing that everyone in the area seemed to always be looking for Quaalude's and needing some extra cash I found a croaker in the tenderloin district who for $10 and a Medi-Cal sticker would write me a prescription for 100 Quaaludes a month. I soon found several others that would do the same.

Before I knew it I had become a one-man Quaalude dispensary selling each Rorer 714 happy tab for a whopping $.50 apiece.

One of the first things that I learned during the early days of my new business venture was this: Quaaludes and Skateboards don't mix. Another thing I learned was that Quaaludes and girls did mix - quite well it seemed - though I wasn't as aware of it as I should've been due to the numbing effects the use of methadone had on my libido.

While methadone did offer freedom from the constant cravings for opiates on one hand, it completely removed your freedom to travel and cast a sort of lethargic pall over your every activity. This was something I was getting pretty damn tired of.

Because of its incredibly addictive nature and its prolonged period of withdrawal - which could last anywhere from six weeks to six months - the quickest and easiest way to get off of the stuff was to simply get strung out on heroin again and then quit that. This, of course, would leave you in the same predicament that you were in before you started methadone. Since I wasn't interested in that, the only other option available was to taper off slowly which could take anywhere from six months to a year to complete. I eventually tapered myself down to 6 mg a day.

I finally left the program almost exactly 5 years to the day from when I started. Aside from the sweats, cold chills, leg cramps and inability to sleep that continued for six months after I stopped, I wasn't feeling too bad.

Three important things happened during the time I was tapering myself off of methadone. My friend Le Roi Jones - who worked with the Tubes - introduced me to a band called Killerwatt that needed a bass player, I met a beautiful girl named Patricia Ngim that I somehow conned into marrying me, and I became obsessively fascinated with seeing how fast it was possible to go on a skateboard before you managed to kill yourself.

Chapter 39

For me skateboarding was a sort of therapy that allowed me to work the toxins left over from the methadone maintenance program out of my system. Whenever I was unable to sleep I would simply put on my clothes and go out and ride my skateboard in the middle of the night until I felt tired enough to sleep.

At first the main aim of these late-night sojourns was to find the biggest steepest hill possible and push as fast and hard as I could up the hill in order to sweat the toxic drug residue from my system. Once I reached the top I'd then ride straight down the hill as fast as I could and then turn around and do the whole thing over again. As the toxins left my system the downhill part of my routine became my main focus.

The first thing I learned was that my boards were too squirrelly to handle the speeds I was attempting to go because of how short they were. This led me to designing and making a series of ever lengthening boards in an attempt to find the most functional size for what I was doing.

Once I found a board that would allow me to go the speeds I wanted, I ran into another problem which had to do with the topography of San Francisco itself.

The problem was this; All the best hills in San Francisco were several blocks long and each hill was broken up by several cross streets that maintained their own flat contours at each intersection. This gave each one of the hills a sort of stepped contour, starting with a steep section that went into a flat section at the first intersection. This was followed by another steep section that went into another flat section and so on.

Now that I had boards that could handle the higher speeds I found that I was sometimes getting airborne coming out of some of the intersections. This really began to pose a serious problem. The only solution was to either stick to the slower hills or design a board that you could kneel down and hold onto while going through the transitions.

This led me to design a 5 foot board with a narrow front and tail area and two pieces of 5 inch long handlebar bend at a 45° angle facing the front of the board - one on each side.

This worked out beautifully with the only problem now being how to keep from getting hit by cross traffic at each of the intersections.

This problem was solved when my only surfer/skater friend - Kevin Claveria recruited a group of renegade 11 to 15-year-old skateboarders to run traffic control during each of the runs.

Most of these kids had to sneak out of the house to come help us because we never started earlier than 10 o'clock at night, which is when the traffic died down in the neighborhood. Some of these sessions lasted until 3 AM.

As time went on the sessions got bigger and bigger as more and more guys came to try their luck on the hill. This went on until the cops finally caught on to what we were doing and tried to put a halt to it at which point we just moved to another hill and continued what we were doing.

In the summer of 1974 a young guy from Japan named Harry Diatoku opened the first skateboard shop in the city of San Francisco and hired me to run the place for him. The shop was located in an area between Union Street and the Marina called Cow Hollow.

Up until the shop opened the only place you could buy skateboard equipment in the city of San Francisco was at Bob Wise's surf shop at the beach.

The skate shop was a converted two-car garage that sat at the end of an enclosed driveway behind an old Victorian house. The entrance to the shop itself was through the garage door - which meant that during business hours the shop was open to the outside air all year round.

Business was so slow when we first opened the shop that my friend Kevin and I got bored and built a skate ramp in the driveway to give us something to do during the day. As word of the ramp got out, business began to pick up due to the influx of kids who dropped by to spend a couple hours riding it.

One particularly dead, though unusually warm day I heard what sounded like an old hot Rod coming up the driveway that served as the entrance walkway to the shop. As I came out the front door to tell the driver that no cars were allowed back there I saw a beautiful lacquer black '47 Chevy low rider with 520s and Astral Supremes come rolling in.

The minute it stopped the driver hit the switch on his hydraulic unit and laid the car flat on the ground. The guy - who had a cast on his leg - threw open the car door, jumped on his skateboard and began riding the ramp. He was a tall thin guy about 6'2" with a short reddish beard and long blonde hair that hung down past the middle of his back.

The guy - who was obviously completely out of his mind - was an airbrush artist/hot Rod painting and lettering expert named Mike Pickel. We instantly became fast friends. That same night Mike joined Kevin and I on our ongoing quest to find out just how fast we could go on a skateboard before reaching terminal velocity.

Up until the time I started working at the skateboard shop, I had no idea who was doing what in the world of skateboarding. As far as I was concerned skateboarding was simply an offshoot of surfing and what I was doing was the skateboarding equivalent of big wave riding.

In early 1975 I met a surfer and skateboard cinematographer from Marin County named John Malvino. John was in the process of shooting a movie about skateboarding called "That Magic Feeling." He was also co-promoting, a huge skateboard contest at the Cow Palace with southern California skateboard promoter John O'Malley.

With John filling me in on what was going on in the skateboard scene and with the reintroduction of skateboarder magazine, I was brought quickly up to speed. John had somehow heard about our late-night escapades and decided to come check things out for himself. He liked what we were doing enough to include it in his new movie.

The first shoot I did with him was during one of our regular nighttime sessions. After the first run he said that it was too hard to see what I was doing and suggested that we tape flares to the back of my board and top of my helmet for the next run.

Someone produced some flares and they were soon attached to my board and helmet with the use of duct tape. Kevin and Mike lit the flares and I headed down the road for my second run.

By the time I hit the first transition I knew I might be in a little bit of trouble because I could feel the flare on my helmet beginning to drop burning material down my back.

By the time I hit the second transition I could feel the material burning through my jacket.

By the time I hit the third transition the jacket had burst into flames and had started melting onto the skin on my back. A second later, I fl ipped the helmet and fl are off my head and attempted to rip the jacket off my back while going over 50 miles an hour down the middle of a street in San Francisco in the middle of the night.

After I retrieved my melted helmet and smoldering jacket, I rode down to where John was shooting. He told me it was still too hard to tell what I was doing and said he wanted to re-schedule the shoot for another time when it was lighter out. I said that was fine with me as long as there weren't any flares involved.

It was through John that I got my first sponsorship riding for Maheraja and met Kim Cespedes, her brother Greg and Nick Van Kriet who also rode for Maheraja. It was also through John that I met two whacked out ex-motorcycle race mechanics named Fausto Vitello and Eric Swensen who over the next 2 1/2 years managed to make me laugh, piss me off, get my picture in a few magazines and nearly get me killed one Sunday afternoon in 1977 in a little town known as Signal Hill…

Mike Pickel and Terry Nails
Photo Credit - Chester Simpson

Chapter 40

I don't know what I was expecting to find the first time I walked into the offices of Ermico, but it wasn't the three scruffy looking guys sitting in an empty warehouse with a set of blueprints for an extremely over engineered skateboard truck, and a refrigerator full of beer that I found.

These guys not only had no product, they had no clue as well. For the life of me I couldn't figure out what the hell they thought they were doing. They didn't skate, they didn't surf and they didn't seem to know anything about skateboarding in general.

The one thing they did have though was absolute confidence in what they were doing. Whatever that was.

Admittedly, the functional design of the truck itself was a thing of sheer beauty. Unfortunately, it was almost totally useless as a skateboard truck. To quote the introductory magazine add:

Stroker Trucks: This is not a truck. The Stroker, designed and manu-factured by Ermico Enterprises, is the latest and most dynamic devel-opment in skateboard steering. In this system spherical joints act upon independent spindles to produce a ride that is the ultimate in speed, versatility and control. The Stroker is adjustable for toe in and toe out, camber, Castor and spring rate. The Stroker is the first in its field because it is in a field by itself…

They certainly were in a field by themselves. They looked great. They were terribly expensive and like I said, they were almost totally useless as far as skateboarding was concerned.

The problem was in the way the system used negative camber while turning. In automotive terms, it goes something like this: "A suspension that gains camber during deflection (turning) will compensate for body roll." This means that instead of remaining perfectly vertical during a turn, the wheels leaned over at a slight angle, giving the wheels a better grip.

This system works perfectly well when used with race compound pneumatic tires that have a pliable surface. Skateboard wheels, however, do not have a pliable surface. This meant that each time you went into a turn the wheels would tip on edge and you would lose the use of most of the flat gripping surface. This also caused the wheels to wear out extremely fast.

The other problem was that it was very hard to adjust how tight or how loose you wanted the trucks to be, because they relied on non-adjustable springs, instead of the rubber pivot pads on traditional trucks which could be tightened or loosened with a wrench.

When the first set of prototype trucks finally showed up I couldn't wait to get them on a board. I had purchased a brand-new hand-made fiberglass Turner slalom board to mount the trucks on. The first problem was that the bolt patterns didn't match up at all which meant that I had to drill 8 more holes in my extremely beautiful expensive Turner. The next problem was that they made a very loud rattling noise and finally, they were so loose that the board was almost impossible to control.

When I told them what was going on with the trucks after the first test ride, Fausto acted like it was my fault that the truck wasn't performing correctly, inferring that I didn't know how to ride a skateboard. Being his usual smart-assed know it all self he grabbed my board and went outside to show me how it was done and totally failed to be able to ride it himself.

After due consideration, a decision was made to replace the existing springs with a set of heavy-duty Harley-Davidson clutch springs. These were not only hard to put in, but also proved to be way too weak as well.

I honestly think that they realized they were in trouble the very first day. However, being as stubborn as they were and having invested so much time and money in the project already, there was no way they were just going to walk away.

The truth of the matter was that if I'd have had a brain in my head, I would've put my old trucks back on my board and grabbed a bus headed towards the skate shop and never looked back. I would have saved myself a whole lot of aggravation and injuries. But where's the fun in that? Besides Eric Swensen and Ed Riggins were great guys. Fausto was okay too - when he wasn't being a smart assed know it all. That, however, wasn't very often.

In the meantime John Malvino scheduled another shoot. He, Kevin, Mike Pickel and I met at the skateboard shop and headed off to film a traffic filled, daylight speed run attempt at my favorite Hill.

Reality checks are always wonderful because of the way they help put things in proper perspective. The best ones come when you least expect them. Now I'm not talking about the kind of reality check where someone has to sit you down and explain some obvious fact of life that you somehow have managed to miss. I'm talking about the kind that you notice all by yourself without the aid of someone pointing it out to you.

Here's my point. All this time I had been designing boards and modifying standard skateboard equipment in order to get the most speed and stability while bombing down these hills and here was John Malvino carrying 40 pounds of camera equipment on a regular skateboard and staying right beside me filming what I was doing while going nearly 50 miles an hour.

It's things like this, and guys like John that have always helped to keep me from taking myself too seriously...

Chapter 41

In the simultaneous parallel dimension that made up the musical side of the universe that I spent much of my time in, I was in no danger at all of taking myself too seriously.

There are as many reasons for wanting to be in a band as there are people who want to be in them. For some people it's about the attention you get. For some it's all about picking up chicks. For some it represents a party lifestyle. For some it's simply a fashion statement.

For me it was a little bit different because I honestly didn't know what else to do. I had grown up with it. It was the only thing my dad ever did and I really never considered doing anything else.

Every one of my family's friends were somehow involved in the entertainment industry. The singer Kaye Star used to babysit my brother and I. We used to go swimming at Phyllis Diller's house. Burt Bacharach and Hal David would go water skiing with us. We called Tex Beneke - the leader of the Glenn Miller Orchestra - Uncle Tex. Uncle Moe owned the Desert Inn where my dad used to work. The Modernaires used to practice at our house. Hell, my Mom was good friends with Irene Ryan and comedian Totie

Fields for crying out loud! It's all I knew. It's all I ever saw and because of it I became part of that rare group of slightly delusional people known as Showbiz Kids. Besides, I figured if it was good enough for dad then it was good enough for me. But that left me with one nagging question: Was I good enough for it?

Killerwatt was a loud hard rock group reminiscent of "The Sensational Alex Harvey Band". It was fronted by a completely insane Scotsman named Ken Cameron, who came from a small town outside of Glasgow called Motherwell. Ken was not only a great singer, he was a great guy as well. He was also a hell of a lot of fun to hang out with.

Ken's partner in the band was a guitar player named George Falbo. It was George who talked me into trying out for the band. Actually he didn't so much talk me into it as simply come over to my house and pick me up and take me to rehearsal with him one day. If I had been left to my own devices, I would probably have never showed up.

While I may have looked like a musician and played an instrument like a musician, I never actually felt like a musician. I still don't. Yes I may have played with a few people that were fairly well-known, but the whole time I was wracked with doubt and insecurity about my playing ability. I was really kind of surprised when they asked me to join the band. Even then I still probably wouldn't have done it. I didn't have much choice in the matter though because George would come by every night and pick me up on his way to rehearsal. I'm really glad he did. It was really a lot of fun and I learned an awful lot playing with those guys.

As my dad once jokingly said to me, "life is just one bad drummer after another." This classic musician's joke also happened to be a pretty good description of what was happening in the drum position in the band - until we met Paul Zahl that is.

After playing with Paul the first time, I realized that I had never actually played with a really good rock and roll drummer before - which is a good part of why I had no real confidence in what I was doing.

Paul was a dynamic madman with near perfect meter and amazing chops and for some reason we just seemed to play perfectly together. I can't even describe it really; it was sort of like magic. Each of us seemed to know exactly what the other one was going to do. We were constantly cracking each other up because no matter how spontaneously bizarre either one of us got, the other one was always right there with him.

While we all loved to play gigs there just weren't many places for new bands to play at that time. The Fillmore and The Family Dog on the Great Highway had both closed their doors in 1971 and the day of the independent promoter was a thing of the past. This left us with dive bars like Jerry's Stop Sign and the Rose and Thistle as the main venues for emerging rock bands in San Francisco.

This changed though when Ness Aquino - the owner of a Filipino nightclub called the Mabuhay Gardens - decided to open his club up to local rock bands.

Paul Zahl (Drums), George Falbo (Guitar), Terry Nails (Bass), Ken Cameron (Vocals), Jesse Bradman (Keybrds) backstage at Mabuhay Gardens

Killerwatt

Photo Credit - Jeff Good

The first two bands that played on opening night at the new club were Killerwatt and the Mary Monday band. Part of Ness' original deal with the bands was that he would feed you and let you keep most of the door money as long as you were bringing in business.

This worked out pretty well for us because, besides being a great front man, our lead singer Ken was one hell of a promoter. Ken was so good at filling the place that during the first year it was open we played the club more times than any two bands combined. This, however, came to a near screeching halt when Ness hired an outside promoter named Dirk Dirksen to take over as booking agent.

With the flowering of San Francisco's punk rock scene and the emergence of the first group of the Northern California punk bands like the Avengers, the Nuns and the Mutants the local club scene began to rapidly change. Particularly at the Mabuhay. Within six months after Dirksen took over, the Mabuhay had become one of the premier punk venues on the West Coast.

After one of our now less than regular gigs at Mabuhay we were approached by Paul Kantner - the founder and rhythm guitarist of the Jefferson Airplane/Jefferson Starship - and asked if we would come open up for his band and the Sons of Champlin at a free concert in Golden Gate Park.

It was fortunate for all of us that Ken was our spokesman and not me. If the job had been left up to me, my response would have been: "Us, open up for you guys in Golden Gate Park? Are you kidding? Hell yes! How much do we have to pay you?"

After asking a few pertinent questions about access to the park for load in and the exact time and date, Ken and Paul Kantner shook hands and we were off to the races or rather Speedway Meadows where the concert was to take place…

5/30/1975 Speedway Meadows, Golden Gate Park, San Francisco CA. The park was crowded, the sky was clear and the weather was comparatively warm by San Francisco standards. The stage was set up on the back of a very large flatbed truck and…

Okay. Honestly I don't remember a single thing about it. I don't even remember being there. If I hadn't actually seen pictures of myself on stage and had all my bass equipment stolen that day, I'd swear I wasn't there at all. It's a total blank.

I found this horribly disconcerting until Ken reminded me that he and I used to drink quite a lot back then. We must have drank a hell of a lot back then because I have almost no recollection of us drinking a lot either! Does that make any sense? Is it possible to drink so much alcohol that you don't remember drinking it? Is a Bear Catholic? Does the Pope shit in the woods? Is the answer to the Ultimate Question of life, the universe and everything really 42? Never mind, sorry...

The one thing that I do remember about the incident was that Paul Kantner gave me enough money to buy all new equipment a few days after the gig. If Paul hadn't already been one of my heroes, he certainly would've been after that.

Sadly all good things must come to an end as the saying goes and Killerwatt and I eventually went our separate ways, though we have all remained good friends.

Chapter 42

Music and skateboarding go perfectly together. But playing music for a living and riding skateboards the way I was is another story. While anyone who rides a skateboard stands a chance of falling and getting hurt - in my case it was a near certainty.

Any fall that I took usually ended with me being rushed to the nearest emergency room with a broken arm or thumb or finger or hand or a combination thereof.

Now if you've ever tried to play bass or guitar with either one of your hands in a cast you'll understand when I say that it is nearly impossible to do it in any efficient manner whatsoever.

It soon became apparent that I was going to have to make a choice between the two because the musical side of the universe started presenting me with more opportunities to be successful than the skateboarding side of things did.

I started thinking about putting a bit of distance between myself and the skate boarding world when I got a gig playing in the Rocky Sullivan band with Nicky Hopkins (Rolling Stones), John Cipollina (Quicksilver) and Greg Douglas (Steve Miller Band).

I should've done more than just think about it because shortly after I got the gig I broke the trapeziometacarpal joint in my left hand - the joint that connects the thumb to the hand. I completely separated my thumb from my hand doing a speed run in the Presidio and consequently had to bow out of playing with the band.

Shortly after this seemingly disastrous event occurred, I got a phone call from my friend Mike Varney telling me about some friends of his that needed a bass player. I sadly informed him that my left hand was in a cast and that I was un-able to play but he thought I should go meet up with them anyway.

A few days later, I got a phone call from a guy named Tommy Heath. He told me Mike Varney had recommended me as a bass player and had given him my phone number. He said Varney had told him about my latest skateboarding escapade and he wanted to know if I could come over and meet up with him and his partner Jim Keller.

I'm not sure what I was expecting when I arrived for our meeting but it certainly wasn't what I found. (didn't I use that line earlier?) These guys looked more like college frat boys than musicians. I'm not sure whether it was because they looked so clean cut and had such short hair or that the guitar player - who had just arrived - was wearing gym shorts and carrying a basketball with a towel around his neck.

I was just starting to formulate a short speech containing a few choice 4 letter words that I was going to recite to Varney the next time I saw him when they started playing me some of the music they had been working on.

Well, the old "you can't judge a book" adage was certainly at work here. These guys were good. Really good! The music they were doing was totally original and very different than anything else being done at the time. By the time they had played me the third song, I only knew one thing. I really wanted to play with these guys.

I got so wrapped up in one of the songs that I picked up a bass and started playing some one finger bass lines. I must have looked pretty funny trying to play bass with a cast on my hand because they both started laughing. They then asked if I'd be interested in joining the band. I asked them if they had a name yet."Not really" they said "Lately we've just been using the name Tommy Tutone" - which was the singer's nickname...

Chapter 43

Shortly after my meeting with Tom and Jim I got a call from Fausto and Eric who told me they had decided to build a skateboard version of a Bonneville Salt Flats type streamliner and that we were going to go for the world speed record at the next signal Hill race.

This presented a slight problem for me. While I really wanted to do the race, I really didn't want to use Stroker trucks to do it. They were just too damn squirrelly!

Stroker trucks had single-handedly managed to elevate the occurrence of speed wobbles from an occasional annoyance to an absolute certainty at high speeds. As far as I was concerned they were a total nightmare.

We tried everything from using ultra-stiff custom-made springs, to stuffi ng the springs with high density polyurethane foam in an attempt to dampen the steering. All to no avail.

The worst part of it for me though, was that it was almost impossible to get it into Fausto's thick fucking skull that the trucks were just too damn dangerous for high speed downhill racing. Every single time one of the new modifications we made to the trucks failed to produce the desired results, Fausto would act like it was my fault for not knowing how to ride them correctly.

Finally one day - after a particularly unsuccessful test run - when he went into his usual "you just don't know how to ride them correctly" routine, I threw the board at him and said "all right asshole, if you're such a fucking expert, then you do it!"

Well, with the smug arrogant look that a fool usually has on his face when he utters those ominous words "hey guys, watch this", he grabbed the board and headed up the hill to show me how it was done. A few minutes later, we all rushed up the hill to see if he had survived the Swan dive he had done into the asphalt some 50 yards down the hill from where he had started...

Things changed pretty quickly after that. Fausto now had first-hand knowledge of what the problem was and he and Eric decided to try out my suggestion that we use a single stroker on the front of the board with a non-turning pivot truck on the back.

Terry Nails and Fausto Vitello
Photo Credit - Eric Swenson

While this did solve the problem of high speed wobble, it was still too squirrelly to use on a stand up board. Since we weren't going to be standing up at the race I decided to call the one guy who knew more about designing downhill speed boards than anyone else, Dave Dilberg.

Dave made a beautiful 5 foot long luge style board for me. It became the main stroker test vehicle.

Next, we started looking around for just the right wheels. The rulebook said that we could use any size wheels up to 4 inches in diameter as long as they were urethane. After months of trial and error a skateboard wheel manufacturer named Power Paw made us a set of 4 inch tall extremely narrow urethane wheels that looked like an oversized version of a modern day roller blade wheel.

Because the wheels had a rounded surface instead of the normal flat surface of a regular skateboard wheel the trucks were now able to function as they were supposed to.

With the addition of a little bit more foam to the springs I now had a board that was not only stable at high speed but was really fun to ride as well.

With the handling problems finally under control, Fausto, Eric and I set about designing and building a monocoque aluminum bodied skate-car for the signal Hill race.

The thing was an absolute work of art. It was about 8 feet long and I laid down in it on my back with my feet facing towards the front of it. Once inside, the opening to the cockpit was covered with a custom-made Plexiglas windshield that was then Seuss fastened into place.

Because of the vehicle's low sleek design, forward visibility was extremely limited and because of its solid metal construction it got incredibly hot inside on sunny days.

The biggest problem we had was trying to figure out how to make the damn thing stop. The design the guys finally settled on was a hand operated rubber tipped single drag brake that came into contact with the ground when activated. It was pretty much the same type used on all soapbox derby racers. The main difference being that their brakes were foot activated and ours was activated by a Harley-Davidson clutch lever.

John Malvino accompanied us on our first high speed test run to film the proceedings. The run took place in the East Bay on a street called Hiller - a long very steep hill off of Old Tunnel Road.

The whole session nearly came to an early end when we were suddenly swooped on by two motorcycle officers who threatened to give us a ticket for speeding and driving an unlicensed motor vehicle on a public street.

When I told them that the vehicle didn't have a motor in it, one of the officers said "if it doesn't have a motor in it, then where was all the smoke coming from?" I said it came from the rubber that was attached to the hand operated drag brake. I told him "look inside of it if you don't believe me."

We explained that the vehicle we were testing was a skate car that was going to be used in a world speed record attempt. The officers were so blown away by the whole thing that they stuck around and blocked traffic for us and timed us with their radar guns for the next three hours.

The fastest speed we got on the skate-car that day was 63 miles an hour with the top speed of the day being clocked at 72 miles an hour during one of the runs I made using the board that Dave Dilberg made for me.

A few weeks later we showed up at the Signal Hill race with tons of confidence and the only skate car at the meet.

Unfortunately, the rain showed up as well. After waiting a few hours to see if it would clear up, the meet was called off and rescheduled.

During the time between the races, Fausto, Eric and I helped design, build and test the undercarriage for a fiberglass skate-car body that Dave Dilberg had built for skateboard slalom champion Henry Hester who was now my only other team member.

When they finally got around to running the contest again everybody and their grandmother showed up with a skate-car.

In the two and half years that I'd been working with Fausto and Eric I had torn the ligaments in my right leg twice, severely fractured my ribs and broken my left hand twice and before the day was over I would end up in the hospital with more broken ribs and a limp that would follow me around for over a year. The worst part of the whole deal was that I hadn't made a single dime during the whole time. Nothing, nada, zip!

Add to that the fact that they held the one and only speed contest of the year on a hill that was a complete joke compared to the hills in San Francisco and you'll understand why I decided that no matter what happened, this contest was going to be my last. It had to be. The injuries I was incurring were doing nothing but keeping me from making a living playing music.

So that was it. Now all I had to do was just get through the rest of the day in one piece...

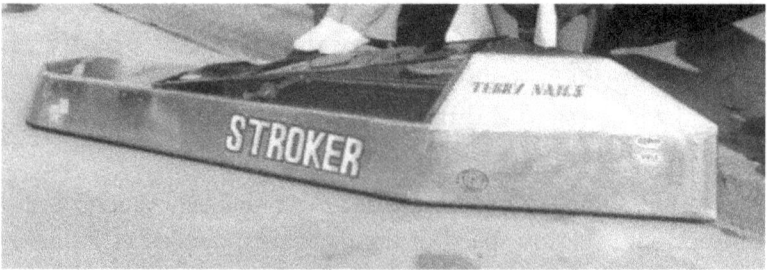

Skate car
Photo Credit - Eric Swenson

Chapter 44

The Saga of Signal Hill

"The merciless rays of the sun beat down on the dry oil rig studded desert landscape of the little Western town known as Signal Hill. Ever since dawn the people from the surrounding areas had begun filtering in to watch the ensuing carnage that would come to be known as bloody Sunday... The contestants, some of whom had come from places as far away as Florida, were gathered there to find out once and for all who was the fastest. Standing among the ranks of the better-known skateboard luminaries was a little-known skateboarder from San Francisco named Terry Nails. As he was getting prepared for his first run, he noticed that the hot desert wind was blowing dirt across the course, causing a potentially hazardous situation. But he went anyway. A few seconds later when he crossed the finish line at more than 55 mph, he realized that he had no chance of stopping because the dirt had made the friction style brakes on his skate-car completely useless. As a safety precaution, a large stack of hay bales had been placed about 50 yards before the intersection. Nails passed through them like a lawn dart through a balloon. He was headed straight for a brick wall on the other side of Redondo Boulevard when he was hit by an elderly woman driving her car through the intersection, causing the skate-car to spin wildly out of control. When it finally came to a stop it was wedged under the front of a pick up truck that was traveling in the opposite direction on Redondo Boulevard. The crowd thought it had witnessed the contest's first fatality" or so the story goes.

Nails & Hester
Photo Credit - Eric Swenson

To be perfectly honest, I don't remember a lot of what happened that day. I was too busy getting ready to watch what was going on before my run and I was too busy riding in an ambulance and laying on a gurney in a hospital emergency room after my run.

Because there had been a bad car accident on the freeway, the doctors were kept so busy that they didn't have a chance to look at me right away. After about three hours of waiting I checked myself out and went back to the hill with a bottle of Jack Daniels and a cane. By the time I actually got back to the race I was so plastered that what little I do remember is a complete blur.

At the end of the race the two guys that I had worked the closest with - Dave Dilberg and Henry Hester - were tied for first place after two or three runs each. I had managed somehow to come in with a second place finish after just one nearly terminal run.

This for all intents and purposes was the end of my career as a professional skateboarder; though not my involvement with the skateboard industry as a whole. I would later go on to develop and head up Thunder Trucks and write articles for different skateboard magazines. It would've been really nice to win but regardless of who actually won the race, I was just glad it was over.

Now I could focus my attention elsewhere…

Japanese magazine shot Signal Hill race
Photo Credit - Eric Swenson

Chapter 45

On the night of January 14, 1978 I was standing on the stage of Winterland setting up my bass rig. The odd thing was that I wasn't even playing there that night. The occasion was the first and last Northern California appearance of the Sex Pistols. I was there setting up my equipment so that my friends Jimmy Wilsey of the Avengers and Mike Varney of the Nuns - both of whose bands were opening for the pistols that night - could use it as a backup in case it was needed.

I'd got to Winterland early so I could set up my equipment without having to deal with the crowds. I had just gotten done setting everything up and was heading towards the backstage area when I came face-to-face with a tall, thin young guy with spiky black hair wearing a black leather motorcycle jacket. I instantly recognized the young guy as Sid Vicious, the bass player of the Sex Pistols. I was a bit apprehensive as he looked me up and down and just stood there staring at me for a minute or two not saying anything. Finally he broke out in a big grin and stuck out his hand and said "hi, I'm Sid." We shook hands and I introduced myself and my wife Patti who was with me.

I wasn't sure what to expect when he first started giving me the eye ball. I mean, I'd heard stories. You know - that he was a complete mad man and that you never knew what he was going to do. I certainly wasn't expecting what he did do though. He turned out to be a very nice guy. I'm glad I got to meet him before all the craziness caught up with him…

That same evening I met a guy that I would end up playing with for several years. A guy I still consider to be one of my closest friends - the band's guitarist Steve Jones.

As far as punk gigs go it was a great show. Things did get pretty crazy as the evening progressed though. It was so chaotic by the end of the gig that Patti and I ended up sneaking the Sex Pistols' drummer Paul Cook out of the venue and back to our house to stay for a couple days till things cooled down a bit.

As it turned out things cooled off completely for the band because the lead singer - Johnny Lydon - quit that night after the show. It was the last gig they ever did with Sid and the last gig they did as a band until they reformed in 1996.

In the mean time I had my own gig to attend to…

Chapter 46

Tommy Tutone was a hard-working Bay Area band that almost no one in town knew anything about. At least not until we put out our first album and started getting national airplay.

In the first three years after we started the band we played at least one gig a week, and sometimes as many as three or four. The reason no one knew who we were was because during that entire three year period I can only remember playing in the city of San Francisco one time and that gig was at a gay cowboy bar called the Red Eye (don't ask).

The majority of the gigs we did took place in the counties of Marin, Sonoma, Napa and Mendocino in Northern California. A few of the places that we played regularly, had originally hired us as a cover band. The truth of the matter was that we never played more than three cover tunes a night. The crowds always seemed to love what we were doing so the club managers never gave us too much of a hassle.

After about nine months of playing together, we got a chance to do a showcase for Clive Davis, the president of Arista records. He liked the band enough to offer us a good amount of operating cash if we would sign a right of first refusal with him. When word of the deal got out to the industry at large, we were quickly approached by several other major record companies. Within a month we signed a deal with the president of Columbia records Don Ellis - who bought out our 'right of first refusal' contract with Arista and gave us a very nice signing bonus.

I immediately spent my portion of the bonus money on a 1951 Chevy power glide deluxe that Mike Pickel and I repainted, re-chromed, equipped with Astral Supremes, 520s and a brand-new set of hydraulics.

I then joined the newly formed Northern California - No. Cal - chapter of *the Duke's Car Club*.

From the time that we signed the record deal, until the time that we started recording our first album, not much changed. Except that I now had a car and I had been forced into opening up my first bank account by our record company. I say forced because not only did I not want to do it, I had no idea how to do it. I had never had a bank account in my life. As a matter of fact I don't think I'd ever actually been in a bank before. I'd never had any money in my possession long enough to be able to put it in a bank before. Fortunately Tawn Mastrey - a good friend of mine who was a Local DJ - took pity on me and accompanied me to the bank and baby sat me through the process.

One night not long after Mike and I had finished installing the hydraulics in my car, I drove up to the little Northern California town of Rodeo where we were booked to play with Bo Diddley. Just as the opening band started to play, I stepped out back for a smoke to find Bo Diddley checking out my car. I went over and introduced myself and we started talking about old cars. We both got in the front seat and I showed him how the hydraulics worked in the car. Thinking that we had at least an hour before we had to go on, I asked if he wanted to go for a ride.

We took off for what was supposed to be a short spin and got so wrapped up talking about cars and telling stories that before we knew it we were cruising the main drag in the town of Richmond -

having almost completely forgotten about what we were supposed to be doing, which was playing music.

Tommy Tutone
Photo Credit - Chester Simpson

When we finally pulled back into the parking lot an hour late, we were confronted by a large crowd of club employees, roadies, managers and band members who looked like they were just about to reenact the mob scene from the first Frankenstein movie.

Fortunately Bo was able to smooth things over and the looks of stern censure that I received when we first arrived, quickly turned to one's of bemusement accompanied by a lot of headshaking. Truthfully any scolding or punishment that I could've received would've been well worth the experience of being able to go low riding with Bo Diddley...

By the time spring rolled around, we had a new manager and a new A & R man named Terry Powell.

Shortly afterwards when Tom and Jim were flown down to LA to do a couple of demos using another rhythm section I should have suspected something was up. I was too busy playing with my car, however, to take any notice.

It wasn't until our drummer, Kenny Johnson was let go that I realized that something fishy was going on. There was absolutely no reason for it.

The truth is that the people on the non-playing side of the music business always try to exert as much control as they can over a project. Usually the results are less than desirable. We should've just stood our ground and told them the fuck off, but being naïve youngsters and not wanting to jeopardize our situation with the record company we did what we were told.

Fortunately, Mickey Shine, the drummer who replaced Kenny was every bit as good and Kenny went on to a much better gig with Chris Isaak.

September found us holed up at the Château Marmont on Sunset Boulevard in West Hollywood, recording at Chateau Recorders in North Hollywood by day, and camped out at the rainbow bar and Grill by night. At least me and my friend Bobby Lingo (aka Sharpe) were.

Bobby lived in Manhattan but had come out to the west coast to see what kinds of new and exciting trouble he could get himself into. I met Bobby on the first night we arrived in Los Angeles, and we were off and running in no time. We got involved in so much mischief together that I'm almost embarrassed to think about it. In truth, I could probably write an entire book about all the insane stuff we got into. Discretion, however, demands that I spare myself the sordid details. It really is quite embarrassing.

While I was relatively drug free, I don't want to leave you with the impression that I was even slightly sober during this time. Far from it. I started my mornings off with frozen Stolichnaya and orange juice and continued imbibing some sort of alcoholic substance throughout the rest of the day until it was time to go to sleep.

I also don't want you to think I was blind drunk the whole time either. I wasn't. Alcohol and I had a weird relationship. It either gave me a functionally operational buzz or made me sick as hell. There was nothing in between. No black outs. No falling down drunk routines. No slurred-out, foot-in-mouth idiot talking. Just buzzed or puking. And I hate puking.

The biggest problem I had with drinking was that at some point during my attempts to keep my the buzz going I would come to the conclusion that drinking just wasn't cutting it and I would start looking for something a wee bit stronger.

So I don't think anyone will find it the least bit surprising that from the time we finished the album, to when we went out on tour, I had managed to get amazingly strung-out again. This time on Persian Heroin. It all started something like this…

Chapter 47

Not long after we finished the album my wife Patti and I were invited to a party at someone's house over in the North Beach area of San Francisco. It was one of those parties that the more upper crust of the decadent crowd seemed to congregate at.

Shortly after we arrived we noticed there was some sort of a commotion going on near the front door that was caused by the biggest human being I'd ever seen in my life. This guy was so big that he had to turn sideways and bend his head down to get through the doorway. When he finally got through the door he walked over and grabbed a large mirror off the wall and dumped a full ounce - of a white powder that turned out to be cocaine - on it and passed it among the large group of party goers. The host of the party introduced my wife and I to the new comer, John Matuszak a defensive lineman of the Oakland Raiders.

Shaking hands with John was an experience in itself. It was like a 1 year old shaking hands with a grownup - my hand being the 1 year old's.

Our host motioned us towards a room at the back of the party were we found several folks smoking something on very thin pieces of tin foil, using straws made out of regular aluminum foil. I had no idea what it was and neither did John but that didn't stop us from trying it when it was passed to us.

If I'd just said no thank you when it was offered to me, I might have saved myself a lot of hassle - but no. After the second hit, I started getting that old familiar foggy feeling that comes from only one thing. I knew instantly that I was going to end up in deep trouble again. The stuff was a very strong, very pure form of smoke-able heroin called Persian.

The worst part of the whole situation was that the guy who brought the stuff to the party was a dealer that just happened to live right next door to me on the corner of Union and Gough. The writing was on the wall. I was screwed and I knew it! And I ignored it to the best of my ability.

After that night John and I hung out quite a bit together. That is until one night about a year later when things got slightly out of hand.

The night started out with us having a few beers at the Palms café on Polk Street. After hanging out there for a couple hours we went across the street and bought some rum and headed across the Bay Bridge to find a party that John said he knew about.

After having failed to find the party and having drunk quite a bit of the rum, we found ourselves cruising along the shore of Lake Merritt in downtown Oakland. It was at this point John decided to pull out his .44 magnum and start shooting at the ducks in the lake as we were driving.

It's never a good idea to shoot a gun from a moving vehicle unless you're in a combat situation. It's even a worse idea to shoot a gun off while driving drunk in the middle of down town Oakland at 9:30 in the evening.

After politely expressing my misgivings about John's spontaneous nocturnal hunting expedition and my continued participation in it, I jumped out of the car and headed for the nearest BART station.

The next day I awoke to find this in the local news paper:

"**Matuszak Arrested** Hayward, Calif. (UPI) - *Defensive lineman John Matuszak of the Oakland Raiders has been arrested on charges of drunken driving and possession of a concealed 44-caliber Magnum and a Bayonet. Matuszak was arrested shortly before 10 PM Monday and released several hours later after his car was spotted weaving down Hesperian Boulevard. He was cited but not jailed, police said Tuesday, a customary procedure for misdemeanor charges. Four officers were called to back up the arresting officer when Matuszak, 6 foot eight and 280 pounds, refused to submit to a sobriety test and allegedly became abusive. Police said they found an open bottle of rum in the car and accidentally discovered the bayonet and handgun concealed under a floormat. Matuszak was the center of attention in New Orleans during Super Bowl week when he broke curfew and was fined $1000 for visiting a French Quarter bar until 3 AM.*"

After I got sober years later, I was privileged to take John to his first 12 step meeting. But I guess I'm not supposed to say anything about that...

A couple weeks after John's Run in with the law I ran into Willy DeVille and his wife Toots at the Old Waldorf. Willy and I had been running partners and friends since the mid 70s when he and another friend of ours named Fast Floyd, had a band called Billy de Sade and the Marquis. I hadn't seen Willy since he had taken the band - now called Mink DeVille - to New York.

Most of the things I'd heard about him in his absence came from articles in some of the rock magazines. During the time they spent in New York the band had honed their playing skills and developed an amazingly soulful, rock and blues sound with just a hint of Spanish Harlem on the side. They also recorded one of the finest first albums I've ever heard in my life called Cabretta.

As Toots and I caught up on the latest gossip I told her that I was in a new band. She asked what the name was and the minute I told her it was called Tommy Tutone she started laughing and went over to Willy and said "Guess what, Terry's in that new band that you really like."

It was kind of funny because he was in one of my favorite bands and now it seemed I was in one of his.

Before too long the conversation was brought around to the subject of drugs and more specifically, where we could find some. After a short trip to my neighbor's house, Willy, Toots and I retired to the Vagabond Inn with a Gibson acoustic, my old dobro and enough dope to keep us all happy for the next 3 of 4 days.

Aside from the occasional breaks we took to eat or get loaded, all we did was sit around and play slide guitar and talk about music for 3 days straight. While I did see Willy a few times after that, I never got a chance to spend that much time with him again...

Terry Nails -Willy De Ville-1978
Photo Credit - Chester Simpson

Chapter 48

After a self-aborted local tour in which we were supposed to open up for the Dixie Dregs - an amazing progressive rock group, that made us look like total fools - we were informed that we had been invited to open up for Tom Petty and The Heartbreakers, with the tour starting in a few days.

Unbeknownst to us, Petty had sent a couple of his crew guys to check us out at a gig we were playing at the Branding Iron saloon in Ukiah California and they liked what they saw.

I received the news with equal amounts of elation and despair. Elation because it was a great tour and despair because I was so strung out that I would have to spend the first couple weeks of the tour kicking dope while on the road.

To help get through this particular bout of self-induced stupidity, I bought 400 little pink Lilly H03 Darvon capsules. I then went to the clinic to beg for as many sleep meds as I could possibly attain legally.

From what I was later told by Dr. Skip Gay, the alcohol I was drinking and the amount of Darvon I was taking should have killed me within the first couple of days. Somehow all it did was make me feel normal - which was all I really wanted.

Because we had been added to the tour on such short notice, we were unable to book a tour bus. We would have to fly everywhere instead which meant that we could be on as many as four different airplanes a day depending on where we were going.

Our First gig of the tour took place at The Red Rocks Amphitheatre in Morrison Colorado, just outside of Denver. The amphitheater itself was built in a beautiful natural rock formation, where concerts were given in the open-air.

While the crowd capacity was fairly small compared to most of the rest of the venues we played on the tour, it was never the less the biggest show we had done to that date. The truth is that we had never played anywhere except bars, so it was vitally important to us that we do as good a show as possible.

This, however, was not going to be an easy task. From the minute we hit the stage Murphy's Law seemed to hit the stage right along with us and in full force. Anything that could go wrong did go wrong. Actually, it started when we found out that we were not going to be allowed to do a sound check - we only got 1 or 2 sound checks during the whole rest of the tour. Consequently, I was totally unprepared for the impending nightmare that was about to happen when we got on stage.

The first problem was that the only monitors working on the stage were the side fills and they were so far away from us that there was nearly a 1 second delay between what we played and what we heard through the monitors. This made it almost impossible to tell who was playing what and when.

The next thing was that my microphone was 35 feet away from my amp but my guitar chord was unfortunately only 20 feet long. When I got to my mic I noticed that my bass seemed to no longer be part of the cacophony of sound being emitted by our back line and the sound delayed stage monitors.

Looking to see what the problem was I turned around and saw that I had inadvertently unplugged myself from my amplifier during my longer than normal journey to the microphone.

If I could've had my choice of any superpower at that particular moment it would've been the power of invisibility because I would've dearly loved to have been able to disappear and just walk off stage.

Sadly I could not, so I did the next best thing. I walked back to my amplifier and plugged myself back in and then walked over and stood right behind our drummer Mickey and sang over his shoulder into his microphone with him, all the while watching his kick drum foot in order to make sure I was playing with him and not the horrible echo coming out of the monitors.

When they finally got the monitor situation semi-straightened out, I had them bring my microphone back and set it up right next Mickey so that I could keep an eye on what he was doing in case something else went wrong.

After the first couple of hectic days of airline travel, I stuffed all of my luggage into a road case on the equipment truck, and traveled the rest of the tour only with things that I could fit in my pockets.

Flying back then really wasn't such a bad experience if you liked that sort of thing, which I didn't. It just wasn't my cup of tea. I wasn't actually scared to fly; I just never found it to be a very comforting experience. It made me nervous as hell to tell the truth. When I get nervous I drink and because we flew a lot, I drank a lot - At least that's the excuse I was using at the time anyway.

My favorite in-flight drink was a vodka martini. I liked them so much that I had a lapel button made that had the words "Vodka Martini" printed on it. Every time a stewardess asked me if I wanted something to drink I would simply point to my button and give her a big smile.

By the time we got around to playing the Pine Knob Music Center in Clarkson, MI June 16th I had stopped taking the Darvon and was feeling as normal as any alcoholic drug addict was capable of feeling which was awful. But at least I wasn't dope sick.

On the evening of July 2nd, after playing at the Augusta Civic Center in Augusta, Maine we boarded a twin engine, prop driven puddle jumper heading for Boston on our way to our next gig at the Ocean State Theatre in Providence, Rhode Island.

Two things about this flight made it unforgettable. The first thing was that the plane was so small that it didn't have a bathroom - which was something that I needed pretty badly since I had drunk an entire six-pack of beer just before we got on the plane - and the second thing, was that it was incredibly noisy because of its propeller driven engines. It was so noisy in fact that the only way that the pilots could speak to anyone, was through the use of an extra set of headphones attached to a long cord that could be passed around amongst the passengers in the cabin.

Aside from my dire need for the use of a bathroom the flight was uneventful until it came time for us to land in Boston. I probably would've never known what happened if I hadn't had the extra set of headphones on when we were setting down.

I was listening to the conversation between the pilots and the tower, when a couple of minutes after we had been cleared for landing, both of the pilots started yelling and cussing at some-body. The conversation went something like this: "Jesus fucking Christ! Who put that idiot down here? Shit! Go around! Go around! No! I think we can make it, I think we can make it!… Fuck, that was close!"

The conversation was accompanied by a momentary touchdown of the wheels followed by an immediate gunning of the engines and an almost vertical liftoff, followed immediately by an almost vertical descent back onto the tarmac and a very short taxi that ended abruptly in the grass at the end of the runway.

I hadn't been fond of flying in the first place, but after this little incident I was positively horrified by it. When I was finally able to speak again, I asked one of our pilots what had happened and he told me that someone had taxied a 747 across our runway right in our landing path. "It's nothing to worry about" he said "stuff like that happens all the time." Somehow, I didn't find his words very comforting.

As we were walking through the airport on our way to our connecting flight we noticed a small group of children sitting on the floor in front of an older gentleman who was himself sitting on the floor and playing an acoustic guitar. As we got closer Tommy and I recognized who the man was at the exact same instant. "Oh my God" I said "it's…" "Pete Seeger!" Tommy said finishing up the sentence. We both sat down on the floor and joined the kids who were listening to one of America's greatest folk legends. Pete was not only one of earliest environmental activists in the country, he was also a dedicated civil rights and free speech advocate, and the inventor of the five string long necked banjo. It was the most enjoyable time I ever spent hanging around an airport terminal…

New York City July 4th… I got my first glimpse of downtown Manhattan at about 3: AM, after having driven straight from the Ocean State Theater in Providence Rhode Island where we had just finished doing a gig.

San Francisco seemed positively rural compared the NYC. I was totally unprepared for the noise, the crowds, the traffic, the steaming manhole covers, the all-night after-hours bars, the all night grilled onion and sausage carts, the stripped abandoned cars that littered the streets, the bondage clubs, the hookers, the easy availability of drugs, the outrageous cost of room service, the bad plumbing, the abandoned buildings on the lower East side, the nonstop partying and the totally insane cabdrivers.

The place seemed like a modern day post-apocalyptic version of ancient Rome - just after the fall. The first thing I learned was that NYC operated on its own time schedule. Each evening's festivities never got started before 11:30 or 12 midnight.

The first day was spent hanging out with my friend Bobby Sharpe (aka Bob Lingo) and trying to figure out where to eat and how to get to the Palladium - where we were told that we might actually get a sound check if we showed up early enough.

The first night's gig went off without a hitch except for one minor incident in the middle of the set. We normally didn't do any cover tunes, but because we were in New York, Tommy decided to do 'Stand By Me' by Ben E. King the former lead singer in one of New York's most famous home town groups, The Drifters. Just before I was to start the opening bass line that leads into the song, I glanced out at the audience and noticed that every single one of the Rolling Stones were sitting in the front row in front of me. I was so astonished that I had a sort of 'deer in the headlights' experience. The next thing I know I hear Tommy clear his voice and ask me what I'm doing. I looked down at my set list which just said 'Stand by' instead of 'Stand By Me' on it and then back at the Rolling Stones and told him that I was just standing by like it said on the set list. "That's Stand By Me" Tommy said. Finally catching on I said "oops, sorry…" and started playing the opening notes of "Stand By Me" and the crowd busted out laughing…

I couldn't wait to go out and see what kind of trouble I could get into after the show. I didn't have to wait long because it arrived at the door of my hotel room about an hour after our 1st nights gig in the form my dear friend and occasional partner in crime Sharon Mitchell companied by Anita Pallenberg the wife/girl-friend of rolling stones guitarist Keith Richards.

Before I could even get out a 'hello how are you' Sharon me grabbed by the arm and said "come on, we've got a limo waiting down stairs. We're on our way to cop, let's go!" Once again I was off and running.

We ended up copping several bags of dope and 3 new syringes somewhere around 1st and Houston before heading right back to my hotel room. We got back to find that the water had been turned off throughout the entire hotel because of a leak in the water main and that there were no spoons or matches to be found anywhere in the room.

Faced with this dilemma, I did the only thing any good dope fiend could do. I called room service and ordered 3 spoons, a glass of water, 5 books of matches and a club sandwich.

It never even occurred to me that this might look suspicious until it actually showed up itemized on my hotel room-service bill. (What kind of hotel lists water, spoons and matches on your room-service bill for Christ sake?)

The next day when Tommy saw me hanging out with Anita Pallenberg and Sharon I honestly thought he was going to have a cow right there in the lobby of the hotel. He pulled me aside and started yelling at me and telling me some story about how a kid who was hanging out at Anita's house had gotten killed and what a bad influence and drug addict she was. I guess he forgot who he was talking to...

I spent the last couple of nights of our stay in New York, hanging out with my partner Bobby at an afterhours club called the Nursery - just a couple of blocks from where we were playing at the Palladium. Years later I was told by Bobby that when I left town I did so in the company of his girlfriend - Ming Toy - who came along with me on part of the tour. I am neither proud, nor have any memory of this. But as Billy Idol once said "that's rock n' roll, isn't it?"

I know... it's a really lame excuse.

By the time I got back home from the tour, I was more broke then I'd been when I left. Things were starting to go south as far as my marriage was concerned and my drug use was once again getting out of hand.

My time with the band came to an abrupt end as well because of what I perceived of as a less than adequate contractual arrangement between myself and the record company. It seemed that some idiot in our management company had decided that Tom and Jim should be the only ones signed directly to the record company, with Mickey and I being signed to a production deal. This basically left Mickey and I out in the cold as far as the decision making process of the band was concerned.

When the full implications of the situation were finally made clear to me, I was so pissed off that I told everybody who may have had anything to do with the deal to "kiss my fucking ass" and promptly quit the band.

I knew that I needed to change the way things were headed, so in a vain attempt to get away from myself, I returned to New York City and imposed myself on my good friend Bobby until my drug habit got so bad that I ended up steeling several hundred dollars from him and was forced to find my way back to the West Coast...

Chapter 49

As I said before, I had already gotten tired of using heroin by 1970 and the last 10 years of struggling with the shit had only made me feel more hopeless about ever being able to get away from it. So in an attempt to find some sort of a solution to the situation, I did the only thing any good drug addict could do when faced with no other options. I moved back in with my parents.

The first thing they did was make me go out and look for work - which I did less than halfheartedly. After a couple weeks of no results my mom presented me with a copy of the help wanted section of the paper. She had circled an ad in it that stated that they were looking for workers down at the juvenile detention center and that they were willing to train the right people for the job.

"Well" I thought, "I've certainly spent enough time down there in the past to know how things operate. What the hell? I'll give it a shot."

After having attended a 3 day orientation class in Reno followed by a couple weeks of academic police training I found myself working the afternoon shift in the main detention center.

I can't tell you how fucking weird it felt to be walking around with a set of keys to that place after spending so much time locked up there as a kid. Even though I was getting paid to be there I still had the feeling that I wanted to escape. I guess it just goes to show that old habits die hard…

After I'd been working there for a few weeks I got enough money together to buy a 1964 Chevy two door hardtop Impala that I immediately lowered and put a set of 520's on. (520s are small skinny white walls tires used on most old school Lowriders).

Not long after I got the car together I stopped to help a young Hispanic looking girl who was having problems with the hydraulics in her lowrider one afternoon on my way home from work. After I got her car started and high enough off the ground so she could drive it, I got in my car and followed her to make sure she made it home all right. When we finally got to her place it turned out to be in a run down trailer park that served as a small Indian reservation called the Las Vegas Paiute Colony.

As I got done fixing the problem she was having with the wiring for the hydraulics a couple guys dropped by to see her. She had just introduced me to her friend Ralph when the other guy who was with him, got this weird look on his face and suddenly pulled out a very large pistol and stuck it in my face. He then started ranting and raving about how he had seen me down at the detention center and that he knew I was a cop. I put my hands up in front of me - palms out and tried to tell him that I was just a counselor at the Juvenile home and that I was in fact not a cop. I even offered to show him the track marks on my arms from shooting heroin, all to no avail.

As I talked to him he seemed to get more and more agitated. Ralph finally told him to put the gun away and stop acting like a fucking idiot. When he refused, Ralph grabbed the gun out of his hand just as he pulled the trigger. Ralph grabbed the gun in such a way that the hammer of the gun came down on the area of his hand between his thumb and forefinger effectively keeping the gun from firing and at the same time pinching the hell out of his hand.

Ralph then pushed the guy - who it turned out was on PCP - into a chair and suggested that it might be a good idea if I got my ass out of there before the guy decided to do something else stupid. I nodding my head, I turned around and walked straight out the door and got into my car and drove away from the place as fast as I could.

Everything happened so fast that I didn't have time to process what was going on. It wasn't until several hours later that I realized just how close I had come to not being able to realize anything else ever again - at least not with this body at any rate.

As it says on the front of the Morton's Salt package "When it Rains It Pours." The same thing also holds true for trouble. Sometimes it just keeps coming once it starts and comes from the most unlikely places.

It was shortly after the gun incident on the Paiute rez that my best friend Steve showed back up in my life. I hadn't seen Steve since we were in Synanon. I soon found out, that he had been pretty busy since then.

Steve had been one of those enterprising individuals known as "drug store cowboys" who supported their drug habits by robbing pharmacies. Specifically, Steve had been known locally as 'the Cowboy Bandit' before he had been busted a couple years before.

Now I'm not sure why, but it never occurred to me to ask him why he was back out on the street so soon after taking such a heavy fall. It also never occurred to me that something fishy was going on when he began showing up with a lot of money and asked me to set him up with a good dope connection. In hindsight it was pretty obvious something was up. But as usual I was in a state of blissful ignorance.

I told him I knew where all the good dope was and that I was quite willing to go get it for him. "But" I said " I'm not introducing anybody to anyone."

After a couple of weeks of him wanting to cop every couple days and trying to get to one of my connections, I let him ride along with me a couple times. Thankfully I never did let him go inside with me when I copped so he never got a chance to put the wire - (bugging device), I found out later - he was wearing to full use.

I had no idea any of this stuff was going on until I awoke one day and glanced at the newspaper to find that everybody that I had been dealing with had been raided by the police during the night.

It was several more days before I found out the extent of Steve's involvement, when one of the people who had gotten raided, showed me a court paper with Steve's name on it.

Why I hadn't been picked up as well was quite puzzling to me. The biggest shock to me was that my dearest childhood friend had become a police informant and had gotten me involved in a situation I wasn't the least bit interested in.

While I wasn't particularly happy about what he had become, I can honestly say that I don't blame him after finding out the circumstances of why he chose to do what he did.

When Steve got busted he had been sent to Carson City Prison - the one I told you about a few chapters back. He was too small and too young to have survived there for very long. He told me some of the stuff that happened to him while he was there and it was really not good. When the police approached him with a deal, he really didn't have too much of a choice. To him it was a matter of survival.

Unfortunately this left me without much of a choice either. It was pretty obvious that the police knew far too much about my activities for my liking. Since I had to come into contact with them on a daily basis at the juvenile detention center, it also became pretty obvious that I should probably find the nearest highway heading out of town if I wanted to avoid any embarrassment at work or possibile future arrest.

The most obvious thing was that the show was pretty much over as far as heroin and I were concerned, though I had no idea how to go about getting out of its grasp.

I'd like to be able to use one of those old closing clichés like "It was nice while it lasted" but it was never nice. It was a total nightmare from the beginning.

Chapter 50

When I finally landed, I came to rest in Santa Monica on a couch in the front room of my friends Michael and Ceanne Herndon. They were great hosts; unfortunately I was a terrible guest - maybe I better make that pest.

I was totally incapable of looking after myself in any sort of normal fashion what so ever when I arrived on their door step. The only way I had ever really been able to support myself for any length of time was either playing music or dealing drugs - neither of which I was capable of doing at the time even if I wanted to.

There is nothing like having a completely dysfunctional drug addict staying with you and eating you out of house and home to put a strain on a friendship. But somehow they were willing to put up with me.

Not long after my unexpected appearance, Michael got me a job working at a large Copy center over on Wilshire blvd where he was employed. The place had been contracted to make copies of every single document and piece of paper - down to the smallest receipt - for a large insurance company who were in the process of moving their headquarters.

Most of the work took we did took place after hours between 9 pm and 6 am every night. The work atmosphere was so lose and informal that it was really more of a fun project than an actual job. It did pay quite well though.

When it finally ended I was put to work on the day shift. It worked out pretty well for a while. That is until I went to lunch with the manager one day who took me a bar and started buying me drinks and then fired me next day for drinking on my lunch hour. You know I've never been able to understand people who do that kind of bullshit.

Not long after I lost my job my girlfriend Donna Gieger from Las Vegas showed up on Mike and Ceanne's door step and we both moved into an apartment over in Venice beach on the corner of Speedway and Paloma a few days later. Living in Venice was a trip to say the least. It's like no other place on the planet. In fact at times it seemed like everybody who lived there was from a different planet.

Shortly after we got settled in I went to work for Nathan Pratt - one of the original Dog Town boys - over on Main Street at the old Zephyr surf shop which was now called "Horizons West." As I dove back into the world of surfing I slipped pretty quickly back into drug use as well. What started out as a fairly healthy obsession soon turned into a drug fueled mania. The early morning surf sessions usually started at around 5 am with 3 bags of heroin and 2 bottles of Miller High Life. Donna saw the writing on the wall and had the good sense to split as soon as she could.

I had been doing this routine every morning for over a year when my upstairs neighbor Kevin - who had just been busted for dealing a heroin like designer drug called Fentanyl - came over and said he would give me a pure gram of the stuff if I went to a court ordered drug meeting with him that evening.

Not being one to look a gift horse in the mouth and being strung out as hell, I readily accepted his offer.

The meeting we attended that evening was held at Cedar-Sinai Hospital over in West Hollywood and it completely changed my life.

I don't know if you believe in coincidences but I certainly don't. I don't believe in them because most of these incidents are just too damn perfect to be viewed as random accidents. As someone once said "Coincidence is what you have left over when you apply a bad theory." I only mention this because the first person I ran into when we walked in the front door was my dearest friend in the world; Joanne Fradkin who I'd lived with in San Francisco. She gave me a huge hug and sat me down in a seat next to her and held my hand the entire meeting.

After the meeting when she told that she had been clean since 1972 I actually cried tears of relief. It was not impossible to get clean and stay clean after all. I had always believed the old adage that said "Once a junky, always a junky" and now I knew for sure that it was not true.

When Kevin and I got back later that evening, I called my friend Sean Coulter up in San Francisco and asked if he still had that extra room in his house he said I was welcome to use any time I wanted to get clean. It took me 2 days to get everything in order and on the following Wednesday I did the last of my dope and had Kevin drop me off at the bus station.

By the time the bus pulled into the station in down town San Francisco I was pretty deeply into the first stages of the withdrawal process - which is not much fun. Especially if you happen to be out in public.

By the time I found my way to Sean's front door I was in no shape to do anything but crawl under a blanket and try to keep from shivering. I spent the next several days lying in a cold sweat doing the best I could to deal with the accompanying cramps and cold chills.

One of the most peculiar side effects of the whole detox shtick is that once I reach the stage of feeling so ill that I am totally incapable of doing anything more strenuous than getting up to go to the bathroom, the whole situation suddenly becomes extremely humorous to me. Yes I feel terrible. Yes my skin is crawling. Yes every smell, sound and bright light is excruciatingly unbearable. Yet I find it incredibly funny that I have inflicted all this unnecessary suffering on myself at the same time. It is clearly very absurd behavior. I mean, what kind of an idiot would do this to themselves? Me! That's what kind of an idiot! And that's what always seems so funny to me.

Chapter 51

A couple weeks later - when I was feeling what I assumed to be fairly close to normal - I went out to Hunters Point to visit Fausto and Eric at the Thrasher magazine/Indie Truck offices.

We had a few beers and I told them why I'd come up to the city. As usual Fausto did the best he could to fuck with me in a sort of good natured way. Good natured for him anyway.

I was just getting ready to leave when Eric asked me what I was planning to do to keep myself busy now that I was clean. "I have no idea" I said. "We have something for you to do if you want" he said as Fausto pulled a set of rough cast skateboard trucks out of his desk and handed them to me.

"They're called Thunder Trucks. We don't really have the time to mess with them right now, but if you think you can do something with the company, go for it."

"What's the catch?" "None" said Eric, "it's up to you." The next day I went out and found a set of small metal skull and cross bones, a skull with a top hat, a dagger and a bat and took them back to the foundry where I molded each one of them on to a different base plate and took them into the casting room to do a test pour to see how well they would come out. They came out great and within a few days we went into full production.

Shortly afterwards, I returned to Venice where Skip Engblum and I set about putting together the new Thunder Trucks team around his main riders Natas Copus, Jesse Martinez and Jim Thiebaud - with John Lucero, John Griggly and Gator coming on board soon after.

Skip and I magazine shot
Photo Credit - Eric Swenson

Running the truck company gave me something to do, but I had no place to live - having given up my apartment in Venice when I headed up north. I once again landed back on Mike and Ceanne's couch and started attending a certain 12 step group's meetings every day in an attempt to stay clean, though I continued to drink beer.

I eventually moved into a small place - four houses up from PCH in Topanga Canyon- with Skip Engblum and Derek von Briesen and began surfing the point every day.

One evening after Derek and I had returned from surfing I was sitting outside in my van staring forlornly at the warm can of beer in my hand when Derek said "You know, quitting drinking is not as big of a deal as you're making it out to be. You've already quit everything else including smoking. You can do it any time you want. You don't even have to finish that beer in your hand if you don't want to." I'm not sure if it was what he said or the way he said it but as I poured the remaining beer out onto the ground that evening I knew with a great sense of relief and certainty that he was right...

I spent the next few years attending 12 step meetings and trying to help other drug addled musicians get over themselves. I did whatever I could to be of service and keep myself busy. I helped put a band together called "As Is" with Ric Gallaher, Rich McHugh and drummer extraordinaire Jan Uvena. I played, wrote, toured and recorded an album with my old friend Steve Jones from the Sex Pistols. I wrote songs with Lemmy Kilmister, Zakk Wylde and Randy Castillo. I recorded an album with a band called Johnny Crash and worked on the 'No More Tears' album with Ozzy Osbourne in the recording studio. I got a chance to briefly work with the Pointer Sisters again and fi nally started my own band with Singer Frank Starr, Drummer Randy Castillo and guitarist John '5' - called Bone Angel.

Left to right, Terry Nails - Frank Starr - Randy Castillo - John 5
Photo Credit - Slow Jimmy

Terry Nails - Taken while playing with Ozzy
Photo Credit - Willia Drew

"We come spinning out of nothingness, scattering stars like dust."
"The universe and the light of the stars come through me."

—Rumi

Chapter 52

On a clear summer evening in 1995 I was sitting on a back porch in Pasadena looking at the stars when I had the oddest sensation that it was not me, but the sky that was sitting there looking at itself from the place I was sitting. Not just the sky but everything. The entire universe was sitting there on that porch looking at itself from the view point of the chair I had been sitting in. All sense of separation between what I normally referred to as myself and the rest of the whole cosmic mish mash, suddenly and completely vanished. The feeling was incredibly peaceful, amazingly bizarre, excruciatingly familiar and at the same time overwhelmingly humorous! So much so, that it was impossible to keep from laughing. The reason I started laughing was because it suddenly seemed so f**king obvious to me that our normal everyday sense of "ourselves" as being separate entities was quite simply just a case of mistaken identity and nothing more!

While this was not the first time I'd had this type of experience, it was certainly the longest and the most intense outside the realms entheogenically/psychedelically induced states of consciousness.

Later that evening it also became clear that I needed to go back and re-examine all those unexplainable events that took place between 1968 and 1970 that I had spent the last 25 years trying to pretend never happened. The problem though was how to go about doing it.

Steve Jones - Terry Nails
Photo Credit - Anita Camerada

Every thorough investigation starts by researching all the information available on the subject and carefully sifting through all the data in order to find information that is not biased towards or against the subject - allowing you to construct an objective point of view. It also starts with knowing where to look. This was my biggest problem. As far as I could tell no one else seemed to have had an experience anything like what I was trying to research.

A look through the readily available information in the annals of brain chemistry and neuro-science seemed to indicate that these types of experiences were the result of the random firing of neurons caused by the introduction of certain psychedelic substances to the brain. In other words they were produced by a sort of random form of mental noise.

Unfortunately this was nowhere near being a valid explanation for the simple reason that they had no actual evidence that this was in fact the case. No one had been able to do any sort of research involving psychedelics since they had been made illegal in 1966, essentially relegating the statement to the realm of pure speculation.

Outside of neuro-science the only literature that I could find that seemed to contain anything remotely like my particular experiences were in the writings of some of the more sophisticated forms of Eastern philosophy. This, however, was not much help because I had no personal access to any sophisticated Eastern philosophers.

The next closest similes I could find seemed to be in the New Age and UFO communities who I did have access to. So putting on my best spiritual/full disclosure seekers disguise, I dove into the murky waters of the New Age movement.

After having attended a couple New Age oriented events I became quite alarmed by the apparent abandonment of the use of critical thinking and the complete disregard for the rules of evidence that were being practiced by many of the speakers and participants. While I did come across some interesting ideas, I was never the less unable to find anything that was very helpful. I did meet some very wonderful and highly entertaining people though.

My next stop took me into the UFO side of the community, though it was pretty hard to find any sort of a line between where the New Agers left off and the UFO investigators began. So much so that I came to the conclusion that, for the most part they were one and the same - with only a very small distinguishable minority existing on the fringes. I pretty much knew I was barking up the wrong tree to begin with because there was an absolute aversion on all sides to the mere mention of the word psychedelics - though in truth some of the things that happened had nothing to do with psychedelics, the New Age or UFOs.

For instance, I woke up sobbing on the morning of December 18th 1986 after having a very vivid dream that my brother Ted had died only to have him actually die in the early morning hours of December 20th less than 48 hours later.

Or like on January 17, 1994 when I casually and seemingly out of the blue asked Toni Drew how well she thought the house we were sitting in would hold up in an earthquake, less than an hour before the Northridge quake struck the area.

Or, when I not so wisely told a friend of mine that he should go straight home and not go out that night, only to have him nearly loose his life in an accident several hours later while he was running around that evening. He was so terrified of me when I came to see him in the hospital that the nurses came in and asked me to leave.

In truth I suspect that each and every one of us gets presented with information of this nature daily, but for some reason we choose to ignore it.

While these are not the only examples of these types of occurrences, they are among the most dramatic. Another reason I knew I was probably looking in the wrong place is a bit more odd because in actual fact the "whatever" and "whoever" I had seemingly been dealing with during those peak psychedelic/entheogenic experiences said very clearly that if I viewed the experiences as being of extra-terrestrial or religious origin or if I tried to put them into any sort of a linear 3 dimensional perspective, I would quite clearly "be missing the point."

Fortunately my investigations were not a total waste of time because they put me back in touch with the Native American community who not only accepted what I had to say, but seemed to know exactly what I was talking about. It also gave me a much better understanding of my grandmother's Cree heritage.

In hindsight, it's quite obvious that I should have just gone straight to the psychedelic community to look for some answers but my years of 12 step program involvement were to preclude that option for the time being. Besides, I had no idea that there still was one. In the meantime, my search lead me to the Philosophical Research Society and then onto the Theosophical Society where I was privileged to have a conversation with Dr. Amit Goswami, former Professor of physics at the University of Oregon's Institute of Theoretical Science and distinguished advisor to the Institute of Noetic Sciences.

Our conversation centered on a series of dreams that we each had been having. I told him about the ones that I had concerning what I had seen and learned in '69 - '70. He in turn told me of a series of dreams he had all of which told him he needed to construct a quantum equation proving the existence of reincarnation. "So what happened?" I asked, "I did it!" he said breaking out in a huge grin. We talked about the importance of paying attention to your dreams and finally about the graph he had been using to explain the phenomena of the disappearance and re-emergence of certain quantum particles. I pointed out that it looked like a normal graph that had been sliced lengthwise down the middle with the bottom of it having been removed to indicate the point where the particles disappeared. He laughed and told me that I was correct and that the missing part was gone in order to show our inability to track the wave function past a certain point. He then explained how it always reemerged back into the realm of the perceivable at a more or less predictable point.

I asked him what I should say to people about the things that I had come to understand about the nature of reality. He said "Don't say anything. But if they ask you, tell them everything!"

As we shook hands, I thanked him for taking time to talk to me. I walked out into the sunshine feeling much better about my quest, though I was still no closer to understanding why what seemed to have happened, had in fact happened...

Over the next few years my quest lead me from Southern California to New Mexico, Wyoming, Oklahoma and the Yankton, Rosebud and Pine Ridge reservations of South Dakota while traveling with a friend of mine who was a Dakota/Lakota medicine man and Sun Dance chief.

During this time I found that while his traditional form a shamanism did involve altered states of consciousness, it was the kind that was brought about through the use of ceremony and physical ordeal as opposed to the use of entheogenically/psychedelically active plant substances.

After nearly 5 years of what could loosely be termed field research, I had a much better understanding of some of the traditional and not so traditional forms of Native American spiritual practices, yet I was still no closer to finding the answers I was searching for regarding my own particular type of experiences.

By January of 1999 my quest had come to a screeching halt and I was at a complete loss as to where to look next. So rather than give to the whole thing up as a bad job, my wife Pam and I moved into a small cabin 20 miles from the Canadian border in Northern Idaho where I began writing about what I had learned during those early experiences in a little book that I disguised as a new age manual called "Conspiracy of Light."

Terry Nails at WFCF radio
Photo Credit - James Cannon

Fast forward to 2011: It's a hot June evening in St. Augustine Florida. The place: the studios of WFCF radio, where I'd been a DJ for the past 8 years. I'd just walked into the studio to visit my buddy Bob Blaize who has a show called the Vanishing Point (that mixes every thing from hookah ballads to speeches on metaphysics and extraterrestrial life) when he began to play a talk by a guy named Terence McKenna.

It's almost impossible to describe how astonished I was by what he had to say. It was the first time in my life that I ever heard someone talk about having the exact same type of experiences with what seemed to be hyper dimensional entities that I had experienced years earlier.

Not only that, but these experiences had instilled in him the same distrust in the so called 3 dimensional scientific model of the universe that they had instilled in me.

For the fi rst time in 40 years of playing hide and seek with what I had seen and learned, I finally knew that I was not the only one who had these experiences.

My elation at finding someone who actually knew something about them was quickly dashed when Bob informed me that Terence had passed away in April of 2000.

When I returned home that evening and related all that I had heard to my wife Pam, she informed me that while Terence was gone, his brother Dr. Dennis McKenna, who was at the very heart of all the experiences Terence talked about, was very much alive. This at last gave me a place to start looking for possible answers…

Chapter 53

After years of being away from all drugs and alcohol through my association with 12 step programs I was pretty apprehensive about ever going back to investigate psychedelics.

Truthfully I had never thought of true psychedelics as being something that allowed you to run away from your problems the way alcohol, opiates and the rest of the normal drugs of abuse did. On the contrary, they had more of a tendency to make you take a very close hard look at yourself and everything else for that matter.

One of the things that the 12 step AA program didn't mention very often was that LSD had a profound effect on its founder and helped expand and refine the original 6 steps borrowed from the Oxford group into its present form of 12 steps.

Bill Wilson, founder of Alcoholics Anonymous, was an avid supporter of the use of LSD to treat alcoholism. Aldous Huxley, the author of Brave New World and The Doors of Perception, introduced Wilson to LSD-25 in the early 1950s. Wilson thought of it as something of a miracle substance because of the way it helped him "Eliminate many of the barriers erected by the ego that stand in the way of one's direct experience of the cosmos and of God."

At one point he even developed a plan to have LSD distributed at AA meetings nationwide.

The main impediment to my personal investigation was fear. Fear that if I took anything what so ever I would shortly find myself back on the nightmare fueled tread mill of addiction.

Fear that I would have to face whatever it was that I came into contact with those many years ago.

The worst fear was that it was an un-reproducible anomaly and that I wouldn't be able to face them. That - for lack of a better term - 'They wouldn't be there if and when I came to call on them.'

If there is one thing I really don't like it's being afraid. Over the years I've become obsessive about dealing with fear the moment it arises. Don't get me wrong. I don't go looking to put myself in fearful situations. I just face them when they show up in the normal course of events. This, however, was clearly not a normal event. Still the fear was there and I really did want to know what would happen.

After doing a lot of research and weighing all the options I decided to keep an open mind and play it by ear if I ever got a chance to try the very short acting psychedelic substance known as DMT.

N,N-Dimethyltryptamine (DMT or N,N-DMT)

A naturally occurring psychedelic compound of the tryptamine family. Its presence is widespread throughout the plant kingdom. DMT occurs in trace amounts in all mammals, including humans, where it putatively functions as a trace amine transmitter. Depending on the dose and method of administration, its subjective effects can range from short-lived milder psychedelic states to powerful immersive experiences; these are often described as a total loss of connection to conventional reality with the encounter of ineffable spiritual/alien realms. Indigenous Amazonian Amerindian cultures consume DMT as the primary psychoactive in ayahuasca a shamanic brew used for divinatory and healing purposes. DMT has virtually no history of use as a "party drug." The effects are so overwhelming and sometimes terrifying that it has never become a popular drug of abuse.

I think it was the "ineffable spiritual/alien realms" that got my attention.

Terence McKenna once gave DMT to a Tibetan Buddhist monk. After the experience was over the monk told McKenna that it brought him to a place the Buddhists had seen many times through meditation. He also stated that it was about as far as one could go into the Bardo - "transitional state" or "in-between state" - and still return to the physical plane afterward.

Considering how extremely rare the substance was I honestly didn't think there was the slightest chance that I would ever come into contact with any DMT, so having to make a decision about whether or not to try it was probably a moot point.

Much to my surprise it wasn't - A moot point I mean. I did, in fact, inadvertently come into contact with a small quantity of N,N-Dimethyltrytamine. Realizing that I may never get another chance I decided to take the jump into hyper –space.

While I am not recommending the use of any psychoactive substances what so ever I do recommend that if you ever decide to try psychedelics 'Do Not Make DMT Your First Experience!'

Someone once asked Terence McKenna if DMT was dangerous and his answer was "only if you fear death by astonishment."

The stuff is almost completely indescribable - though I'll do the best that I can…

The first thing that happens is that you hear and feel a slight buzzing. At the same time the light begins to change and everything takes on a soft glow as if lit from within and you begin to see everything become crystal clear and incredibly symmetrical. This all happens in the first 10 seconds.

Next your body, as well as the entire sensory realm, begins to fragment into an intensely buzzing field of amazingly beautiful bright colored psychedelic fractals. You are now making the jump into hyper-space. This all happens in the first 20 seconds and it's not a particularly comfortable sensation.

The experience sort of reminds me of a line from "The Hitch-hikers Guide to the Galaxy" were **Ford Prefect** says:

"you better be prepared for the jump into hyperspace; it's unpleasantly like being drunk."

ARTHUR DENT:

Well, what's so unpleasant about being drunk?

FORD PREFECT:

You ask a glass of water that!

It's at this point things get even weirder. You are now in hyper-space and it's like nothing you've ever seen before and yet for some reason it's staggeringly familiar.

You have now reached the 30 second mark.

Suddenly you're in what seems like a cartoon version of a Marks Brothers movie drawn by the artist Alex Grey that's being played in reverse at 5 times the normal speed. It's almost like being in an extremely humorous very busy clown infested cosmic carnival midway. Why it should present itself like this is beyond comprehension.

At this point you have to be very careful not to give way to uncontrollable laughter or you're liable to miss the rest of the journey.

It's in this realm that people begin to bring back reports of encounters with all kinds of entities. Interestingly these entities all seem to be aware of your presence long before you become aware of theirs. It's here too that many people seemingly come into contact with groups of entities who begin cheering for them when they arrive.

For me this time there was no cheering. Just a simple 'Welcome' once I had passed through the cartoon realm. Here I was again in the same beautifully jeweled psychedelic light realm that I'd visited so many years ago.

When I asked why there was no cheering the entities laughingly said "it wasn't very helpful last time was it?"

"But what about the elves" I asked. "The elves are for Terence" they said.

I then asked about the Green Lady that so many people had reported seeing and they said "Do you really need a green lady?" We all started laughing.

Knowing I didn't have much time I began to ask a lot questions. I said that all I wanted was to bring back enough information to make sense of my earlier experiences.

"Everything you want to know, you know already. All you have to do is relax and remember" I was told.

I felt like someone who had been groping around in a dark room for years and suddenly found a light switch.

Memories and understanding came flooding back. I now understood why this realm seemed so familiar. It's the place we come into and go out of as we transition in and out of this experiential realm.

I also understood that there is no death. The idea of death is something peculiar to this realm only. It actually doesn't exist.

I could also clearly see that the seeming physical world is not anything like we think it is.

When I asked why everything seemed so complicated they said "if it wasn't so complicated, you wouldn't believe it was real."

I also understood how fear and ego helped concretize the illusion of separateness thus allowing us to have the particular type of experience we call everyday reality.

I was then shown that we have all had a hand in setting up this entire experiment from the very beginning and how very ingenious the whole thing is.

At this point I began to feel myself backing out of hyper-space. The whole way back in I could clearly hear the voice saying over and over again "remember, remember, remember…"

When I finally arrived back in this world I glanced at the clock and saw that I'd only been gone about 15 minutes though it felt like a life time and a half.

The next couple times I tried it the same thing occurred except the cartoon type entities had now begun asking how I was enjoying my earthly experience so far. The implication being that our experience of everyday reality is something like a cosmic carnival ride.

Finally on the 5th jump after spending what seemed like an eternity on the cosmic midway a very clear calm voice asked me "have you had enough yet?" Yes I have. "It's nice to see you again but you really don't have to keep doing this. You know you can't go any farther than this." I realized that I had known this for a while but had been unable to remember it once I had backed out.

One of the problems with DMT is that it's extremely hard to retain the information you gather for any amount of time once you're back. Knowing this I set up a recording device beforehand so that I could keep a record of the experience.

For me the experience gave me a little bit of closure and a better understanding of those earlier experiences. While DMT was very helpful in my case I do not recommend it to anyone who doesn't at least have a hundred hours of serious psychedelic flight time under their belt. It's not something you want to play with.

Psychedelics should always be approached with deep respect and much careful preparation. They can be great tools of exploration. They can also cause serious problems when used in a frivolous manner.

"Reality is merely an illusion, albeit a very persistent one."

—Albert Einstein

Chapter 54

So far the story has been a sort of biographical romp through the exterior landscape of my life. Now you are about to get a glimpse of the bizarre thought processes that make up the interior landscape inside my head. This, for better or worse, is what my internal dialog sounds like most of the time.

The main question I've been asking myself and anyone else who'll listen is this: **What the hell is going on here?** What is this thing that we loosely call everyday reality? I don't know about you but it certainly doesn't seem to be anything like what our society and science would have us believe it is.

One of the main impediments to finding out the answers to our most fundamental questions about the nature of reality is that we don't actually pay close attention to what seems to be in front of us. Instead our minds are focused more on our linguistically framed conceptual notions about what we're looking at than what we are actually seeing in the moment.

A perfect example of this is how we always seem to fall in love with the image of a person that we have created in our own minds and not the actual person themselves. This is why most love affairs end so badly and why our current notions of reality are likely to end in the same way.

Another problem is that our popularly accepted notions of reality are firmly rooted in outmoded concepts put forth to us by 19th century materialists who believed that the only thing that existed was "matter" (or energy) and that all things are composed of material and all phenomena including consciousness are the result of material interactions.

This may have been a viable theory 200 years ago, but a quick glance through the annals of modern physics shows it to be a completely untenable notion.

The greatest impediment to finding out what's going on here is a little harder to explain because of the problems that present themselves when trying to construct an overall view from within any given self-referential system. Our generally accepted three-dimensional concept of reality is one such system.

The thought goes something like this:

Any closed self-referential system is incapable of completely defining its own axioms from within its boundaries because of its total reliance on the data that is available from within the system itself. Unless that system is capable of constructing or obtaining a view of itself from outside of the system, the data regarding its true nature will be of limited value because it is essentially incomplete. In basic terms it is incapable of fully knowing itself because it has nothing to compare itself to.

In order for this type of investigation to take place you have to at least allow that there is another possibly valid point of view from which to observe things.

Sadly this is something that western culture is not quite ready to admit.

This is because the main function of culture is to set forth and maintain a set of rigid boundaries that define what the proper acceptable behavior is for any given member of a society. From the stand point of the culture these boundaries are essential and necessary for the general populace to adhere to in order to keep the basic structural integrity of the group intact.

However, they are functional and valid only up to the point where the members of the society they are meant to help govern begin to become more psychologically sophisticated than the earlier culturally defined boundaries allow for.

It is in this situation and on this particular precipice that Western culture now seems to be teetering. The behavior of Western society as a whole is not only psychologically unhealthy; it is also dangerously irresponsible in its attitude towards the planet. At least this is what seems to be happening from the stand point of a moderately aware semi-evolved ape type person firmly rooted within the objective confines of a 3 dimensional view of reality.

But from the standpoint of the psychedelic world something else entirely is going on.

Chapter 55

"Your unexamined assumptions are what dictate your experience of reality"...

"The Light is your protection, the darkness your teacher, when you truly understand this you will realize that there is no darkness and you need no protection"...

I'm not sure why, but the preceding lines of information are the sort of things that one comes away with from a psychedelic experience. While I will grant that they don't necessarily come from hyper dimensional entities - though they sure do their best to present themselves that way sometimes - they very clearly don't seem to be the product of the random firings of neurons coupled with chaotic phosphene activity (mental noise) either. For me, neither the neuro-scientific explanation of these occurrences nor the religio-spiritual explanations fi t or serve the situation very well. They do, however, fit within the western cultural point of view quite well and it's our attachment to that cultural point of view that is part of the problem. You see, if we going to make any headway concerning the question of "what the hell is going on here" we need to be able to at least temporarily overcome that attachment.

As the French philosopher Simone Weil so aptly put it "Attachment is the great fabricator of illusions; reality can be attained only by someone who is detached."

The same thing applies to belief and skepticism. A determined skeptic can be just as unscientific as a determined believer.

According to the most sophisticated forms of Hindu/Buddhist philosophy as well as psychedelically gathered information, we must set aside all notions about what we think or have been told about what's going on here and look at it as it is in the moment. What we think it means to be human and all conceptual notions about the subject/object, spiritual/material, self and other relationship we have with reality. Only when we are capable of doing this will we have any hope of seeing things exactly as they are.

So what is it that the psychedelic world is trying to tell us? How does it occur?

To begin with it depends on what and how much you take. In this particular instance I'm referring to the substances that affect the 5HT2-2a serotonin receptor sites in the brain only such as LSD, DMT, Ayahuasca and Psilocybin.

The communication itself can take place in several different forms. It can be as simple as having a personal revelation or a deep intuitive knowing. It can take the form of a spectacular visual demonstration. It can even take the form of a dynamic participatory experience or just a straight forward face to face question and answer session with what Terence McKenna liked to call the "other". (This can be quite disconcerting if you are not prepared for it.) At times it seems telepathic and as I mentioned earlier in the case of DMT you just seem to clearly remember exactly what the true nature and purpose of this maze like structure we call reality is.

This, to me, was one of the most truly astonishing and comforting experiences of all.

Once again I'm not here to try and advocate the use of any particular thing, substance or technique, nor am I here to try and tell you what's going on.

The truth of the matter is that I don't know. Nobody does. Not science. Not religious leaders. Not anyone. Reality is a very subjective and personal experience. Ultimately it's up to you to decide what's going on. My aim is simply to relate a few observations.

First off, the infinite universe of time and space that we are aware of is just a tiny slice of an overall consciously dynamic self aware universe that - for lack of a better term - seems to be peopled by many different conscious entities, all of whom operate and exist at different frequency/dimensional levels.

While all of these so called dimensions - including our own - have a seeming physical existence they are much more akin to being a type of virtual reality world than anything else. The same is true for our experience of having a physical body as well.

Interesting and very cutting edge experiments have recently been conducted by Professor Mel Slater at the Event Lab for Neuroscience and Technology at the University of Barcelona Spain that have been able to demonstrate that body ownership can be transferred to an entirely computer generated virtual body or avatar through the use of immersive computer technology. The Experimental Virtual Environments Lab for Neuroscience and Technology (EVENT Lab) explores the interfaces between virtual reality, neuroscience and psychology, in order to exploit scientific understanding of the human brain and behaviour and use this knowledge to construct enhanced virtual reality systems (www.event lab.org).

The most intriguing theory I've seen regarding the nature of reality so far comes from Dr. Brian Whitworth of Massey University, Albany, Auckland, New Zealand

In the opening paragraph of his paper "The Physical World as a Virtual Reality"

Dr. Whitworth writes:

"This paper explores the idea that the universe is a virtual reality created by information processing, and relates this strange idea to the findings of modern physics about the physical world. The virtual

reality concept is familiar to us from online worlds, but our world as a virtual reality is usually a subject for science fiction rather than science. Yet the world could be an information simulation running on a multi-dimensional space-time screen. Indeed, if the essence of the universe is information, matter, charge, energy and movement could be aspects of information, and the many conservation laws could reduce to a single law of information conservation. If the universe were a virtual reality, its creation at the big bang would no longer be paradoxical, as every virtual system must be booted up. Ultimately, whether the world is an objective reality or a virtual reality is a matter for science to resolve. Modern information science can suggest how core physical properties like space, time, light, matter and movement could derive from information processing. Such an approach could reconcile relativity and quantum theories, with the former being how information processing creates space-time, and the latter how it creates energy and matter".

Further on in his paper Dr. Whitworth writes:

"In the virtual reality conjecture, physical reality is a processing output, not something that exists in itself. The evidence presented for this view is from science not religion, e.g. the physical matter we generally take as "reality" is only 4% of the universe, with dark matter (23%) and dark energy (73%) the rest (Ford, 2004, p246). If most of the universe isn't the world we see, why assume the world we see is all there is? Indeed, how can a finite physical world created by a "big bang" a finite time ago conceivably be all there is? http://brianwhitworth.com/VRConjecture.pdf

This is one of the most fascinating cutting edge scientific papers to come along since Niels Bohr published his model of atomic structure in 1913. Unfortunately, it so cutting edge that most scientists will have a hard time taking it serious enough to look into it.

The implication that the Universe is a sort of self-programming virtual world is intriguing, if only as a thought exercise. It raises some particularly interesting questions: If it's a program, can it be hacked? More importantly has it already been hacked? That would certainly explain a lot of the inconceivably bizarre bullshit that goes on here.

At the interactive level, the psychedelic experience tells us that everything that we see is simply a virtual projection that we have created for ourselves that we are capable of entering and clothing with the perception of solid materiality.

This is made possible by the fact that we have no memory of what went on preceding the time we found ourselves in this world, making it easier for us to believe the consensually agreed-upon self-limiting information we find when we get here.

Essentially what we have here is a kind of multi-level virtual Leisure World that can function as either a learning tool, a cosmic intelligence test, a setting for your own heroic journey or a multidimensional cosmic horror film.

Ultimately, you choose how it plays out though, while you're here, it is very unlikely that you will remember this.

Couple this with a few well placed Morphic Behavioral Fields (*see Rupert Sheldrake*) and there you have a self-limiting virtual reality world in which to get lost in.

Our belief in our own separate existence and its ultimate reality - along with the self-limiting linguistic structures through which we perceive the world - are what keep the game in play in its present form for most of us. Couple this with the common fear based notion of self-preservation and voila! Here you are reading this right now!

Whether any of this is true or not, I cannot say for sure. I do know that we have no chance of finding out unless we are in the very least, able to allow for it as being possible.

At this point I'd like to bring in Dr. Dennis McKenna.

Dennis McKenna is an ethnopharmacologist and has studied plant hallucinogens for more than 30 years. In 1975, he co-authored the book Invisible Landscape, with his brother Terence McKenna. The book was based on their investigations of Amazonian hallucinogens in 1971. He also acted as co-star of his brother's book True Hallucinations, which further described their experiences while in the Amazon.

Dennis went on to study the botany, chemistry, and pharmacology of ayahuasca and oo-koo-he, which he wrote about for his thesis work. He earned his Master's degree in botany at the University of Hawaii in 1979 and his Doctorate in Botanical Sciences in 1984 from the University of British Columbia. Since that time, he has conducted extensive ethnobotanical fieldwork in the Peruvian, Colombian, and Brazilian Amazon.

In 1990, he joined Shaman Pharmaceuticals as Director of Ethnopharmacology and in 1993 he joined the Aveda Corporation as Senior Research Pharmacognosist. In 1998 Dennis co-founded the non-profit Institute for Natural Products Research (INPR) to promote research and scientific education with respect to botanical medicines and other natural medicines. He is a founding board member of the Heffter Research Institute, serves on the Advisory Board of the American Botanical Council, and has served as a board member for Botanical Dimensions.

After years of having no one that I could talk to about my experiences I finally got up enough courage to get in touch with Dr. McKenna and tell him my story and to ask him the question I'd been asking myself all these years, "Just what the hell is going on here?" Here in part, is his response:

So what the hell is going on? Well, I wish I knew, to be honest. Like you, I've puzzled over these experiences all of my life. I have three theories, and I'm not sure how to test them. And they all sound pretty crazy.

1. There really are other dimensions 'out there', wherever that is, higher vibrational level or whatever, and they are populated with a whole menagerie of strange entities, and you can break through the barriers that normally separate our dimension from that other dimension; you can do this with high doses of psychedelics under the right circumstances and for some people. There may be other ways but that's the only one that's worked for me. And you can connect with those entities and that other world. Now if this theory is true, it pretty much overturns everything we thought we knew about the world and reality; everything science has taught us and most of the rest of human knowledge (although there are lots of hints from other traditions). This is the very real world that shamans explore daily; for them it's just the way things are. And if you talk to them about it, they will say, 'well, of course. What did you think was going on?' So you have the option to just abandon your Western scientific rationalism and accept that this is how it is.

2. The alternative explanation, which some may see as a cop out, is that it has to do with our brain architecture and the way that the brain processes information. What we experience, our subjective experience, is **not** *reality; we know this, neuroscience tells us this. What we experience as reality is a model of reality that our brains construct. A hallucination if you want to call it that, and we have this hallucination and live inside of it and choose to call that consensus reality. Everybody lives in more or less the same, consensually shared hallucination. I tell my students sometimes, this is the 'serotonin' hallucination; we're all high on serotonin all the time. But if we tweak the brain processes that are generating this hallucination, by substituting a psychedelic for serotonin, we can step out of it and experience a different reality. It's kind of like changing the channel on your TV set; tweak the neurochemistry in just the right way and you tune into a different channel. You see the world differently much like putting on colored glasses or something like that. Everything looks different!*

3. The third possibility is that it's a combination of these two. There really is another dimension out there, inhabited by all sorts of entities, and that built into our brain architecture are structures (the serotonin 2A receptors, the main target for 'classical' psychedelics) and when you activate them, you see things about the world that normally just do not surface to conscious attention, because they interfere with everyday functions, like survival. So you only see them under special circumstances, when you're in a position to pay attention. Normally they are there, but suppressed or ignored, because they are not related to your immediate needs to navigate in the world.

I have no idea if any of these proposed explanations are true, or if there are other explanations I haven't thought of (no doubt there are!). I'm not sure how you would go about testing or verifying them. I'm not sure what to 'do' about them, if anything. For me personally, I deal with it by reminding myself that we really know very little, about the way the world is, the way our minds work, and everything else. Science makes us arrogant; we like to think we know a lot. Actually, we don't know shit! And maybe that's the point. Maybe the lesson to be learned from these experiences is a lesson in humility. Always keep in mind the limitations of our knowledge, these experiences are forceful reminders that we don't know much of anything. We're monkeys, after all; why should we know anything?

*I don't know if these words are comforting for you or just frustrating, or maybe just lame, but they are honest. If I've learned anything from psychedelics and from 61 years of life, it's that we really don't know much. As JBS Haldane said, "the world is not only stranger than you suppose, it's stranger than you **can** suppose", seems like he was right.*

OK, I'll go with that. Maybe one of these days, maybe when we die, it will all be explained to us. I hope so, cause I'd sure like to know. You and I are not the only ones who would like to know.

All my best,

Dennis

Well, I guess if I had to pick one of the three theories I'd have to go with theory number one based on my own personal experience. Numbers two and three seem to make more sense from the standpoint of the standard three-dimensional model of reality and, it's precisely for that reason I picked number one. You see, ever since that first night in Muir Woods I've had a very hard time taking the standard three-dimensional model of reality very seriously.

The one thing that I've learned is that if I believe in anything as being a particular way I will never be able to see it for what it truly is. This is because the act of believing itself is a self-limiting process. It precludes anything that doesn't fit within that belief system as being possible. Belief is not an option when searching for ultimate understanding.

Someone once said "Life is a mystery to be lived not solved." I don't entirely agree. I suspect it is a beautiful livable mystery that can be solved, but only by those who live it to the fullest.

What's going on here? I honestly don't know. It sure is beautiful though!

Whatever it is it's certainly not what we've been told it is.

So how do we go about finding out what's going on here? As far as I've been able to figure out it goes something like this:

- "Pay attention to what's going on in the moment."
- "Keep an open mind."
- "Don't adhere to or reject anything in particular."
- "Learn to think outside of the box."
- "Don't take your illusionary ego based self seriously."
- "Ask lots of questions."
- "Listen to your intuition."
- "Follow your own path."
- "Explore hyperspace."
- "Hangout on the edges."
- "Push the boundaries."
- "Take note of recurring patterns no matter how off the wall or unimportant they may seem" - you might learn something.

And as a hyper dimensional being once said to me:

- "Have no Fear"

But most importantly of all:

- "Have Fun with what you're doing... whatever it is!"

And if you can't manage to do any of that, make sure you get yourself a good pair of tennis shoes... You're gonna' need 'em!

www.ingramcontent.com/pod-product-compliance
Lightning Source LLC
Chambersburg PA
CBHW022005080426
42733CB00007B/483